Praise for

Counseling with Choice Theory

"I appreciate Dr. Glasser's elaboration on the theme of creating satisfying relationships in our lives. I particularly like the existential emphasis on the roles of choice and responsibility. This book reinforces the notion that we do have choices and that we contribute to our degree of happiness by how we think and act in our present-day living."

—Gerald Corey, Ed.D., ABPP,
professor of human services and counseling,
California State University, Fullerton

"William Glasser is a brilliant therapist, and he has written another brilliant book. The case-study format that he has developed with this work allows the reader to feel as though he or she is experiencing and participating in the therapy sessions. . . . Dr. Glasser writes like a novelist, playwright, or short story author, but most important, he clearly explains the basic precepts of choice theory and reality therapy, and shows the reader how these constructs can be used in real therapy sessions to help real people change their behavior and their lives."

—Gary G. Forrest, Ed.D., Ph.D.,
clinical psychologist and executive director,
Psychotherapy Associates and
the International Academy of Behavioral Medicine,
Counseling, and Psychotherapy, Inc.

"'It is what you choose to do in a relationship, not what others choose to do, that is the heart of reality therapy.' This quote perhaps best summarizes Dr. Glasser's break from external control psychology and emphasis on choice and responsibility. This book focuses on relationships and provides insight into the mind of one of psychotherapy's giants. The pragmatic writing style allows one to not only learn about reality therapy but also about life."

—JON CARLSON, PSY.D., ED.D., ABPP,
distinguished professor of psychology and counseling,
Governors State University

"Taking an unromanticized look at our modern phobias and manias, Glasser offers sharp insights into how making rational, effective choices can heal the mind and soul."

—*Publishers Weekly*

"In this age of managed care . . . reality therapy might be a better alternative to expensive psychiatric drugs."

—*Library Journal*

Counseling with Choice Theory

Counseling with Choice Theory

The New Reality Therapy

William Glasser, M.D.

Foreword by Peter Breggin, M.D.

Quill

An Imprint of HarperCollins*Publishers*

A hardcover edition of this book, titled *Reality Therapy in Action,* was published in 2000 by HarperCollins Publishers.

First Quill edition published 2001.

Designed by Nancy Singer Olaguera

The Library of Congress has catalogued the hardcover edition as follows:

Glasser, William.
Reality therapy in action/William Glasser.—1st ed.
p. cm.
ISBN 0-06-019535-5
1. Reality therapy. I. Title.
RC489.R37G547 2000
616.89'14—dc21 99-31691

ISBN 0-06-095366-7 (pbk.)

01 02 03 04 05 ❖/RRD 10 9 8 7 6 5 4 3 2 1

To the three women in my life who have contributed
their love, energy, and brain power to keep reality
therapy alive and well all over the world: Naomi Glasser,
Linda Harshman, and Carleen Glasser

Contents

Acknowledgments

It goes without saying that this book is a joint production by Carleen, my wife, and myself. She edits, suggests, comments, corrects the copyedited manuscript, and reads the galleys for accuracy. Her contribution is invaluable. But her work I take for granted; we do everything together. What is different about this book from all my other books is the assistance and support I got from Albert Ellis. In May 1999 we were both invited to present at a conference in Boston on internal control psychology. Before the conference, he took the time to read *Choice Theory*, which is my contribution to this expanding subject. While he did not agree with all of it, he agreed with a lot of it and wrote a long paper based on this book, which he presented at the conference. We were together for two days, and we had a chance to get acquainted.

At the conference I told him about this book, which was already with my publisher, and asked him if he would read it for a blurb. He not only read it, he took the time to go through it page by page and dictate his comments onto an audio tape. I appreciate what he did, and I have incorporated almost all of his detailed suggestions into this book. I also sincerely appreciate the blurb he gave me for the back cover. I look forward to accepting his invitation to visit and, perhaps, to present at the Albert Ellis Institute the next time I am in New York City.

Literally hundreds of people are deeply involved in the work of the William Glasser Institute. They teach and promote the ideas of choice theory, reality therapy, and quality schools all over the world. It is to their credit that the ideas have spread so far and so fast since their beginning in the early 1960s.

Finally, I appreciate the monumental work of Dr. Robert E. Wubbolding, Professor of Counselling at Xavier University in Cincinnati. He has recently completed a scholarly book on reality therapy that needed to be written. Called *Reality Therapy for the 21st Century*,[1] it includes the history, the research, and the multiple applications of this therapy that is so important to students studying the field of counselling.

---

1. Robert E. Wubbolding, *Reality Therapy for the 21st Century* (Philadelphia: Taylor and Francis, 2000).

Foreword

Thank You, William Glasser

Thank you, William Glasser, for casting light on the darkness that psychiatry has shed over the landscape of our minds and spirits. This book is a beacon that can lead people into the brighter land of fulfilling relationships based on personal responsibility and conscious choice.

Nothing has harmed the quality of individual life in modern society more than the misbegotten belief that human suffering is driven by biological and genetic causes and can be rectified by taking drugs or undergoing electroshock therapy. Modern psychiatry has made up the most ugly story possible about human conflict and emotional pain—reducing it to nothing more than bad genes and unbalanced chemical reactions. If I wanted to ruin someone's life, I would convince the person that biological psychiatry is right—that relationships mean nothing, that choice is impossible, and that the mechanics of a broken brain reign over our emotions and conduct. If I wanted to impair an individual's capacity to create empathic, loving relationships, I would prescribe psychiatric drugs, all of which blunt our highest psychological and spiritual functions.

Life has no meaning if we fail to see that the good life is made of loving relationships. Life has no hope if we do not know how to live by conscious decision making based on sound principles. To take responsibility for ourselves, rather than to control other people, is one of these principles. To offer ourselves, rather than to criticize and carp, is yet another.

William Glasser tells us with absolute clarity that happiness and fulfillment depend on the quality of our relationships, that choice determines the kind of relationships we have and will have, and that controlling others is not the way to get what we want. He dramatically illustrates these truths with the imagination of a playwright. Although he speaks less directly about it, his stories confirm that a caring, empathic relationship lies at the heart of any kind of therapy.

As infants we were made of the relationships that nurtured or failed to nurture us. We didn't choose our parents and other caregivers, but within a few years we began to make choices about how to react to them. As adults our choice of relationships determines who we are and who we will become. Dr. Glasser puts these concepts together—relationship, responsibility, and choice—in a powerful, unique fashion.

The distinctive and unique aspects of Dr. Glasser's approach should encourage therapists to find their own viewpoints and methods, and inspire clients to search for the therapists who meet their needs. However, Dr. Glasser does much more than embody genuine individuality; he communicates about the universal. His therapy focuses on choice making—the central aspect or core of human experience. Dr. Glasser promotes each client's ability to make his or her own decisions—to become consciously autonomous, or self-directing.

Dr. Glasser himself, as well as his "clients," come alive on the pages of this book. In Chapter One, we watch him offer therapy to one of his clients, who reminds us of the character Melvin Udall, played by Jack Nicholson in the film *As Good As It Gets*. The client gets the kind of counseling that results in a more real ending and a genuine new beginning for someone with obsessive-compulsive disorder. If you've bought this book but haven't seen the movie *As Good As It Gets,* rent or buy the video and watch it first. Then start Chapter One for an entertaining and enlightening trip into the world of psychology—and into yourself and human reality. From the child who hates his teacher and the teenager who loves sex to the man who wants a sex-change operation, you will be entertained and enlightened by Dr. Glasser's approach to both the ordinary and the extraordinary in human relationships.

Dr. Glasser's therapy is based on inescapable truths: Meaningful relationships are central to the good life, the choices we make will determine their quality, and we can create them only if we take responsibility for ourselves without controlling other people. His vivid stories and dialogues brilliantly illustrate how to go about creating a good life.

Peter R. Breggin, M.D., Director, International Center for the Study of Psychiatry and Psychology. Author, with David Cohen, Ph.D., of the 1999 book, Your Drug May Be Your Problem: How and Why to Stop Taking Psychiatric Medications.

Preface

In this follow-up to my 1965 book, *Reality Therapy*,[1] I invite you to sit with me in my office as I practice the latest version of this therapy with a variety of clients. What I provide are large segments of individual sessions but rarely a verbatim transcript of a complete session. I focus on the essential interactions: the places in the sessions where I intervene as I attempt to persuade clients to make better choices. I demonstrate a variety of techniques that have proved to be effective, many of which have evolved since I developed the therapy thirty-five years ago. I also reveal what is going through my mind as the counseling proceeds.

On the basis of my 1998 book, *Choice Theory*,[2] I contend that we choose essentially everything we do, including the behaviors that are commonly called mental illnesses. Although I explain how this concept of choice applies to every client I see, it is still a radical idea. But it is not a totally new idea. In *Reality Therapy* I agreed with Thomas Szasz,[3] that mental illness, as it was understood then, did not exist. What existed in 1965 was a theory of mental illness that was based on Freud's explanations of unresolved, unconscious conflicts. Contrary to that belief, I contended in *Reality Therapy* that clients were not sick. They were responsible for their behavior and should not be labeled mentally ill.

Even before 1965, there were therapies that deviated from

Freudian doctrine. An example, rational emotive therapy, now called rational emotive behavior therapy, created by Albert Ellis, is still widely practiced. Since reality therapy, many other non-Freudian therapies, too numerous to mention here, have gained acceptance. What has yet to gain acceptance is my continuing belief that it is wrong to label people mentally ill.

Since 1965 when I wrote *Reality Therapy*, Freudian dogma has been replaced by a new theory of mental illness based on biochemical causation, but the concept of mental illness remains intact. Contemporary mental health practitioners now explain that mental illness is caused by an imbalance in the chemistry of the brain. The new organic psychiatrists claim that drugs are the best way to correct this imbalance.

What I still believe, and describe in detail in this book, is that the organic causation of mental illness is no more accurate than the Freudian argument. What is labeled mental illness, regardless of the causation, are the hundreds of ways people choose to behave when they are unable to satisfy basic genetic needs, such as love and power, to the extent they want.

Psychiatrists, who used to be trained to do psychotherapy, now mostly prescribe drugs. In a sense the present psychiatric thinking is that patients' symptoms have little to do with the way they choose to live their lives. In *Choice Theory* (see Chapter Four), I refuted this biochemical causation as strongly as I refuted the idea of unconscious conflicts when I wrote the earlier version of *Reality Therapy*. In this book I demonstrate that when clients begin to make better or more need-satisfying choices, the symptoms disappear. Brain-scan research shows that the brain's chemistry changes to reflect these more effective choices.

In his 1991 book, *Toxic Psychiatry*,[4] psychiatrist Peter Breggin cites research to support his statement that mental "illnesses" like schizophrenia, depression, manic-depressive (bipolar) disorder, panic disorder, obsessive-compulsive disorder, and attention deficit disorder have never been proved to be genetic or even physical in origin. To quote from the cover of his book, Dr. Breggin believes that therapy, empathy, and love must replace the drugs, electroshock, and biochemical theories of the "New Psychiatry."

Although Dr. Breggin may practice psychotherapy differently from me, we are both firm supporters of the idea that people, no matter what their diagnoses, can be helped to live their lives more effectively through psychotherapy. I join him in his concern that brain drugs, while useful in some instances, are overprescribed today. I urge you to read his 1991 book, as well as his more recent books, which further explain his ideas.

In this book I quickly focus on what I believe is the source of almost all clients' problems: the lack of satisfying present relationships. Frequently, I use the term *disconnected* as another way to describe these unsatisfying relationships. I contend that it is this disconnection that leads not only those in need of counseling, but all of us, to *choose* the painful, destructive behaviors that are commonly called mental illness, crime, and addiction.

I realize that the claim that we choose essentially everything we do is a huge break with current thinking. But I back up this claim by the way I counsel every client in this book. Furthermore, I am prepared to demonstrate the validity of my thinking by working with actual clients in front of an audience in any psychiatric teaching hospital anywhere. I say this because I have done it, and I am more than willing to do it again.

In this book you will be there with me as I counsel. I ask you to judge the effectiveness of what I do either from the standpoint of a therapist or that of a client. I invite therapists to think of what you might do if you were counseling the same client that could be equally or more effective. And I ask those of you who have been in therapy, to compare what I did with what you encountered in your treatment.

As you will clearly see from my running comments, choice theory is on my mind all the time. I don't believe that anyone, even with formal training, can practice reality therapy if he or she is not thoroughly familiar with the content of the book, *Choice Theory*. If you decide to read *Choice Theory*, prepare for what many readers have told me: The book is easy to understand yet deceptively complex. It has many layers, and each reading can take you to a deeper level of understanding.

What *Choice Theory* makes crystal clear is that when 99 percent of the people in the world have difficulty getting along with someone else, they use an ancient, commonsense belief I call external control psychology. This controlling, punishing, I-know-what's-right-for-you psychology is the source of the unsatisfying relationships that afflict so many people's lives. The more it is used in any relationship, the more the relationship is harmed and, eventually, destroyed. I believe this psychology is a plague on humanity.

This means that almost everyone who comes or is sent to a therapist is suffering from his or her use of external control psychology or someone else's use of it on them. Unless they learn a new psychology, the same or equivalent to choice theory, therapy has little chance of success.

What you will see in every chapter is my present reality therapy approach. What I now try to teach clients, which I had not yet developed in 1965, is to give up external control psychology and replace it with choice theory, or to learn to use choice theory to defend against the use of external control psychology on them by others. I usually integrate this teaching into the therapy, and my clients may not even realize what I am doing. But if I believe a formal explanation of the theory will help, I give it as well.

Although I introduce enough choice theory so that you can follow what I do as I counsel, I have not attempted to rewrite *Choice Theory* here. If you want to get the most from this book, you should read both *Choice Theory: A New Psychology of Personal Freedom* (1998), and *The Language of Choice Theory* (1999).[5]

---

1. William Glasser, *Reality Therapy* (New York: HarperCollins, 1965).
2. William Glasser, *Choice Theory* (New York: HarperCollins, 1998).
3. T. S. Szasz, *The Myth of Mental Illness* (New York: Paul B. Hoeber, Inc., 1961).
4. Peter Breggin, *Toxic Psychiatry* (New York: St. Martin's Press, 1991).
5. William Glasser and Carleen Glasser, *The Language of Choice Theory* (New York: HarperCollins, 1999).

Counseling with Choice Theory

1

Jerry

. . . it is what you choose to do in a relationship, not what others choose to do, that is the heart of reality therapy.

In the movie *As Good As It Gets*, the lead character, Melvin Udall, portrayed by Jack Nicholson, is a textbook illustration of what is known as the mental illness obsessive-compulsive disorder, over which he has no control. But, following choice theory, I do not believe that Melvin is suffering from a mental illness or that he has no control over what he is doing. I believe he is choosing to obsess and compulse to deal with what is so obvious from the beginning of the film: He has no satisfying close relationships. To have any chance to lead a rewarding life, he, like all of us, needs at least one satisfying relationship.

When we fail in the effort to connect with other people, as Melvin surely has, we suffer because the need to do so is as much built into our genes as the need to survive. Almost all the pain or abnormality associated with the choices that are commonly called mental illness are a genetic warning: We are not involved in a relationship that satisfies what our genes demand.

When we suffer any pain, mental or physical, our brain does not let us sit idly by and do nothing; we must try to do something to reduce the pain. What is called mental illness is a description of the ways in which huge numbers of people, such as Melvin Udall, choose to deal with the pain of their loneliness or disconnection. In Melvin's case, the choice is mostly to obsess and compulse, a choice so commonplace it has been wrongly labeled a mental illness for at least a hundred years.

But, inadequate as obsessing and compulsing (or any other symptom we choose) may be to help us reconnect, it is always our best choice at the time to fulfill one or more of five needs built into our genetic structure: survival, love and belonging, power, freedom, and fun. At the moment we choose any behavior, we believe that any other choice would be less effective; what we choose is the best choice at the time we choose it. When we say we shouldn't do it and then go ahead and do it, we suspect it won't be effective—but not enough to stop us from choosing to do it.

Choice theory explains the whole mechanism of genetic needs, the pain associated with their frustration, and the choices we make to deal with this frustration. In this book that theory is put into practice as reality therapy. I have been teaching and continuing to improve this method of counseling since I first developed it in 1962. In 1965 I wrote the book *Reality Therapy*, a method of counseling now taught all over the world.

But the 1965 book did not have a theoretical base; this book explains that choice theory is that theoretical base. It includes many improvements over the original, an important step in keeping the process current. For variety, throughout this book I use the terms *counseling*, *therapy*, and *psychotherapy* interchangeably because I believe they are different ways of describing the same activity.

As stated, to cope with the pain of his disconnected life, Melvin is choosing an assortment of obsessive and compulsive behaviors that are his attempt—often unsuccessful—to restrain the anger that he immediately chooses whenever he has to deal with people he finds frustrating. When the movie begins, he seems unaware of this anger and its danger to both himself and others. But he surely knows that he, like all of us, needs love and belonging because he plays a character who writes bestselling romantic novels.

His symptoms are classic for the compulsive person he chooses to be. Melvin is so afraid of germs that he uses a new bar of soap each time he washes his hands, and he washes them many times a day. He also has a compulsive routine he goes through each time he locks and unlocks the four locks that secure the front door to his apartment. But the most obvious of his symptoms is the huge effort he makes to avoid stepping on cracks, which in a city like New York is almost a full-time occupation. He is also a particularly nasty man who verbally abuses anyone who frustrates him.

In a believable way, the movie shows him trying to relate to Karen, a lonely single mother, played by Helen Hunt, who is burdened with an asthmatic seven-year-old son. Karen maintains a strong front, but it is clear that she sees her life going down the drain socially and sexually. Even before they get involved, Karen knows a lot about Melvin. She is "his" waitress in a restaurant near his apartment where he eats every day and where he is both obnoxious and weird whenever he is frustrated, which is almost all the time. For example, Melvin brings his own sterilized plastic tableware; he won't use the knife, fork, and spoon the restaurant provides. And he insults anyone who is sitting at "his" table when he comes into the restaurant to eat. He doesn't care about the awful scenes he creates.

In a short time Melvin and Karen fall in love. The movie ends happily with Melvin and Karen in each other's arms. His choice to obsess and compulse has diminished to the point where it is implied that he and she have a good chance for a normal life together. Again, in fiction, love conquers all. But don't get me wrong, I like happy endings. I wouldn't want the movie to end any other way.

As we walked out of the theater, I said to my wife, "I give that relationship a week before they start having serious problems." In my mind the best hope for Melvin is psychotherapy.

Without a good relationship with a skilled therapist who is able to teach him that other people matter, the happy ending will be short-lived. And it was obvious that Melvin did not have anything like this necessary relationship with the psychiatrist depicted in the movie.

About six weeks before I saw this movie, I received a call from a new client, Jerry. As I describe my extensive work with Jerry, you will realize why I became so interested in Melvin. If you have not seen the movie, rent the video, and you will see what Jerry saw: Melvin seems to be living his life.

Jerry called for an appointment on a Thursday morning. I had a full day booked, but he was so insistent on the phone that I told him he could come at six when my last scheduled appointment was over. I didn't ask him what his problems were or anything else because I prefer to find out what I want to know in a face-to-face session. I did tell him that if it was needed, we could have more than an hour, since no one was scheduled after him.

From his voice I surmised that he was an unhappy middle-aged man. But even before I saw him, my knowledge of choice theory told me much more. I knew that his problem was caused by a present, frustrating relationship. But what people like Jerry and Melvin don't know—and don't want to know—is that the behavior they complain about is chosen and, in most instances, is harmful to any relationships they may have. Instead they tend to blame their unhappiness on other people or on a mental illness over which they have no control, usually both.

What almost never occurs to them is that they themselves are responsible for what they are feeling and doing. Getting across to clients the message that it is what you choose to do in a relationship, not what others choose to do, is the heart of reality therapy.

From his urgency I was also sure that Jerry was choosing some symptomatic behaviors that would interfere with his ability to establish the satisfying relationships he needs. And from his demand to see me as soon as possible, it was unlikely that he was depressed. People who choose to depress are rarely as demanding as he was; depressing is a choice that immobilizes us. Whatever Jerry was struggling with, he didn't come across as immobilized, but he did seem to be in a lot of pain. I didn't think of obsessing or compulsing, but they certainly fit the situation.

I also knew that by the end of this first session, I would be able to discover the unsatisfying relationship that is the source of his pain. I can't remember ever failing to find this out, usually early in the session.

The only way I can help him is to teach him to reconnect if he has someone he wants to be close with, or to connect if he has no one. The way I work is to help him relate to me; he can use what he learns with me to relate better to the other people in his life. The more I focus on the symptoms he is choosing—the obsessing and compulsing—the more he will cling to them and blame me for not being able to rid him of them, as if I have some psychiatric magic to make them disappear. In practice I can only guide him toward learning that he has choices and then using this knowledge to choose to reconnect. If he does, the symptoms will disappear. But with people like Jerry and Melvin, this is a big if.

Because print has only one dimension, what can't be shown in the therapy transcripts that follow is the tone of our voices, the expressions on our faces, and the pace of the conversations. Therefore, there is always the possibility that what may have seemed too confrontational or too passive on paper could, in practice, be good counseling. My explanations as I proceed should help with this potential problem.

I had barely started with my last regular client when I heard the waiting-room bell chime; someone was there. I assumed it was the new client and thought he must be really anxious to see me. The client I'd just started with remarked, "Maybe you ought to see who that is; the person seems to be too early to be the next client. It might be some kind of emergency."

The way my office is set up, there is a waiting room that enters into an anteroom, and from that small room through a door into my office. When you leave you go directely out into the building from the anteroom. This way the clients have privacy in and out.

I went out, closed the door to my office, and opened the door into the waiting room. It was the client who had to see me. He was a middle-aged man, I'd say about fifty-five, glasses, sparse hair, and very well dressed. He stood up when I opened the door, and he was very tall, at least six five, and must have weighed well over two hundred pounds. As we introduced ourselves, I reached out to shake his hand. At first he hesitated and then gave me a very reluctant shake. We introduced ourselves, and he apologized for being early. He did thank me for letting him know that I'd heard the chime. I wondered about the limp handshake, but I didn't have to wonder long. What was wrong was immediately apparent an hour later, when I let him into my office.

Instead of coming right in, he just stood at the door staring at the interior of the office. He waved his hands at me as if to say: It's okay, don't worry, and said: "Doc, go back and sit down, I'll come in in a minute. I just don't rush into strange rooms. When you get to know me, you'll understand."

I went back to my chair and simply watched. He looked all over my office, especially at the furniture, the carpet, and the pictures on the wall. We have a lot of small earthquakes in Los Angeles, and pictures often get crooked. I hadn't noticed mine were, but he did and immediately went to all four pictures and carefuly straightened them out. Next he went over to a small, not very comfortable chair with a plain covering and moved it alongside the more comfortable client chair by my desk, carefully avoiding the lines on the carpet, which wasn't easy because he had big feet.

While he was doing this, I could see his face working as if he had to get everything in order before he sat down. When he finally took a seat in the plain, uncomfortable chair, he relaxed, and his face broke into a big smile that seemed to express: *Now that I'm more in control of the situation, I feel comfortable*. I didn't say anything. If I acknowledged his obviously compulsive behavior, I would be giving it more importance than I think it's worth and tacitly promising that I could do something about it. Jerry didn't mention what he had done and looked to me to begin.

I began innocuously with, "Would it be all right if I call you Jerry? I'm more comfortable with first names. If you want you can call me Doc like you just did; I like to be called Doc. He said, "Fine, call me Jerry. Everyone calls me Jerry."

"Okay, now that you're here, let's get started. It'll help me a lot if you'll tell me why you called?"

"Tell you why I called? For Christ's sake, doctor, are you blind? I can't even walk across a room like a normal person. First I had to straighten out your pictures; how can you stand crooked pictures? Then I had to avoid all the lines in the carpet and, while it looks comfortable, I couldn't sit in the regular chair. I don't sit in chairs with patterns in the fabric. This chair is fine."

This hostility was the first of many challenges from Jerry. It was his way of trying to get me to understand that he had to go through his compulsive routines because he was suffering from a mental illness and couldn't help himself; that my job was to get rid of his craziness for him. But since I know that what he has shown me is the way he chooses to deal with unsatisfying or nonexistent relationships, my focus will be on his relationships, especially, in the beginning, his relationship with me. The way he behaved would make it very difficult for him to have friends, and I tended to doubt that he was married. I started in by saying, "Good, you're seated. I saw what you did but I'm sure you've been behaving like that for years. Something besides how you enter a strange room brought you here today, and I wonder what it is. We have time; I'd like to hear some of the story."

With this statement I gave him some credit for knowing

that what is really wrong goes far beyond his symptoms. This is a technique I use to avoid getting bogged down in them. Doing much more than acknowledging his symptoms is a waste of valuable time. "But you've got to admit, what you just saw was pretty crazy."

"I've seen crazier, but I'm not here to debate the extent of your craziness. But something happened recently in your life that you can't handle. I wonder if you'd tell me what it is."

When I said that his face lit up with a big smile. He was comfortable with what I said, especially, that I didn't think he was so crazy I couldn't help him. That smile told me that he was beginning to relate to me, a very important task for this first session.

"Doc, you're right. There is something. But I want you to know that there's a lot besides what you saw here. Remember how reluctant I was to shake your hand. It's because I'm so afraid of germs I wash my hands all day long. I've got three locks on my front door and on the door from my garage. My back door is nailed shut. I lock and unlock all three of those locks at least four times every time I go in and out. Just checking; you can't be too careful. And even when I'm home, which is a lot, I keep checking those locks all day long. But the worst is the way I walk. It doesn't happen very often, but when it does it's really nuts. Look, I'll show you."

He got up from the chair and walked around the office carefully avoiding the lines in the carpet. It took him quite a while because what he did was take one step backward for every two steps forward. While he did it he smiled and said,

"I like to walk that way. When I'm home, I do it for an hour or two when I've nothing else to do. You must have guessed I live alone.

"Not completely alone—you've got all those crazy things you do. They keep you company. Meeting you is like meeting a crowd."

"You don't take these things I do very seriously."

"Do you?"

"Of course I do. Would you like to be this way?"

"No, I wouldn't."

"Do you think I could just stop?

"You seem to have stopped now. Whatever you're doing, I'd just keep it up. But that's up to you. I don't want to talk about it anymore. I want to find out why you're here."

It's important not to get trapped into talking about the symptoms, to send the message: *I'm not interested in your craziness.*

"Doc, do you have any idea what I do?"

I looked at him as if there were no way I could know what he did.

"I'm a screenwriter, a successful one. I make a good living at it. I'm well-known in the business. When I sit down to write, all my craziness melts away. I write all kinds of movies, but I like love stories best. Not sex, Doc, love. You can take a kid to see my movies."

"I still want to find out why you're here."

"I'm here because of a new movie that's coming out. In fact it's out this weekend. I saw a special showing of it about six weeks ago at the Directors Guild. It's going to be hot; everybody's raving about it. It's got Jack Nicholson in it, he plays a crazy guy called Melvin Udall. But they could just as well have called the character by my name. I mean Melvin Udall *is* me. It's uncanny. The cracks, the locks, the hand-washing, the whole nine yards. If you want to know more about me, go see it this weekend. It's called *As Good As It Gets*. All the people I know are starting to call me Melvin. They're good natured about it but I can see why they do it. Melvin is a nasty guy; you know how nasty Nicholson can be on the screen, he's a grade-A son of a bitch. You know what he does in that movie? He lives in a big New York apartment, you know one of the really big ones on the West Side. He has a gay artist for a neighbor and he hates him. I mean, this Melvin guy hates everyone, until he meets the girl. Anyway, the gay guy has a cute little dog, and Melvin actually picks him up and throws him down the trash chute. If that dog hadn't come out okay, I think the people in the theater would have torn down the screen."

"Are you a nasty guy?"

"I have my moments; he's not nasty all the time, either. What's different from the movie is my neighbor's cat. For some reason that cat has taken a liking to me, and I can't get rid of him. As soon as I step outside there he is, rubbing up against my legs."

"How does the movie turn out? Does the guy stay crazy or does he fall in love with the girl and get cured?"

"Of course he falls in love with the girl and gets cured. I wish it would happen to me."

"I have a feeling it has happened to you. But it's not coming out as well as it did in the movie. Is your craziness getting in the way? The girl, Jerry, the girl. Tell me about the new girl in your life."

"How do you know it's a girl? You haven't seen the movie."

"You just said, 'Melvin gets the girl and I wish it would happen to me.' If I'm wrong tell me."

"It was that movie. It happened at that movie. It made me sad. What happened to Melvin at the end of the film is never going to happen to me. In real life, girls run away from crazy guys like me."

You can see how hard it is for people like Jerry to face the fact that they're lonely. Prying information about this woman out of Jerry was like pulling teeth.

"Can you tell me, Jerry? I'm waiting."

"Doc, here it really gets scary. On the way out of the movie I met Carol. The woman in the movie is called Karen; it's almost too much of a coincidence. But that's not all. Go see the movie, you'll know what I mean."

"I will this weekend. But, please, tell me about Carol?"

"We walked out together, I was really sad. She's beautiful, and I was attracted to her. I turned to her, just naturally, not to pick her up or anything, and said something like, 'Great movie,' and I noticed she was teary, like she'd been crying. When I saw those tears, my heart jumped—that movie had affected her. She saw the good in Melvin; underneath all his schtick, he's really a good guy. And here she was walking out of the theater with a carbon copy of Melvin himself. I said, 'You're crying, what's wrong?' And she said, 'You've got tears in your eyes, too.' And I did, I was really affected by that movie and then meeting her. All I could think of was to say, 'Would you like to go down the street and get some coffee.' She said she'd love to. Doc, it was like a miracle. There we were in Starbucks on Sunset, drawn together by that movie. We just sat there and talked and talked. She works a jillion hours a week, but I've been seeing her two, three times a week for the past month a half. I think I'm in love with her."

"Did you tell her about the coincidence?"

"I had to tell her. My God, I carry my own silverware. Not plastic, good stuff—see, here in a case."

He showed me a small leather case of silverware, he had it in his inside jacket pocket. It was so clean it sparkled.

"When we went into Starbucks, I took this out, I needed a spoon for my coffee. When she saw that she looked right at me and said, Doc, I couldn't believe my ears, 'Would you be as kind to me as Melvin was to Karen?' I mean my craziness didn't turn her off. I think it turned her on. Melvin was a nasty, crazy nut, but underneath it all she saw a kind, loving nut."

"What did you say when she said that?"

"I said, 'Would you take a chance with me, like Karen did with Melvin?' She said, 'Let's talk,' and we talked for two hours. And it was a little like Melvin was with Karen the first time they went out except we didn't kiss. We sat there, eating and drinking, and I forgot to use my silverware. I'd put it back in my pocket, and I never took it out again."

"You were there two hours—what did you talk about?"

"We talked about the coincidences. I told her about my life, that I'm a successful screenwriter; remember Melvin wrote romance novels and he was successful. He had a nice apartment, I have a nice home in West LA. I told her that my craziness doesn't affect my work, that I love to write. And that I love music, I play the guitar, just like Melvin played the piano. I told her about my total failure with women, that I'd really given up on them until I saw that movie. She couldn't understand that, because we got along so well and it's hard to explain. It's that whenever I'd get close to a woman, I'd start getting real crazy and it's finito.

"You told her that?"

"I decided to tell her the truth. Karen knew Melvin was crazy; it was in the movie; you'll see it. And it didn't stop her. It's hard to describe how I felt that night, lying to her didn't even cross my mind."

"But the craziness has happened with her, that's why you called me."

"No, not yet, I've been pretty good. It's like the movie. We get along pretty well. I told her all about myself. We do a lot of talking when we get together. I've told her about all the movies I've been involved with. She's been to my house, she's even let that cat inside. I thought I'd go crazy—cats shed—but it didn't bother me. It's that we're getting along so well, that's why I'm scared. I don't want to lose her. You've got to help me."

At this point I knew something was seriously wrong with Jerry. Maybe the something that was causing him to choose all his crazinesses. It had to do with Carol, but it'd been going on for a long time before Carol. Something I don't think the movie could have handled. But I'll see the movie and find out about that. What I want him to tell me about now is Carol. All I know is she's beautiful and very lonely. I said,

"Jerry, I want to help you. I think I can help you. But before I get into what may be wrong, I'd like you to tell me about Carol, Describe her, you're a writer, the more I know about her, the more I think I'll be able to help you."

"She told me her whole story. It's a lot like Karen's in the movie. Well, we don't really know that much about Karen but we do know she was a single mother. Carol is a single mother, too. I don't want to spoil the movie for you, but Carol's daughter is older, she's in college and she's doing well. The problem is money. College is expensive and Carol's broke. She gives all she can get her hands on to the kid. She sells makeup at a department store, Robinson May. She also makes women up; she goes to their houses before parties. She's forty years old, and when she's made up she's a knockout. And she's a widow. The guy she was married to abused her and the kid. She feels guilty about that. It was hell for twenty years. The guy was a drunk, but he always made a good living and she had some money; she didn't have to work. But he had the bad habit of drinking and driving. Two years ago he was killed in an auto accident; it was his fault and two people in the other car were killed, too. He had no license, no insurance, nothing. She was wiped out. She lost her home, her car, everything but the clothes on her back, and she can't get her life together financially. She works all the time. She's pretty much given up on men. And on sex, too. She told me that that first night. We haven't had any sex, I hold her for hours at a time. I don't care if we never have sex. I just don't want to lose her."

"She hasn't threatened to leave you, has she?"

"No, not at all. I just feel it won't last. I've never been as close to anyone as I am to her. You can see why I'm so upset, can't you? I don't think I'd want to live if I lost her. Sometimes I get the idea I ought to kill myself now while things are so good. I'm not going to do it; I just want you to know what's going through my mind."

"Jerry, I don't want you to lose her either. I don't even want to talk about you losing her. I want to see that movie, and I want to think about what's gone on here. I think this's enough for today. But she knows you came to see me, doesn't she? You say you tell her everything."

"That's no problem. I told her I wanted to get some help for my compulsions. She thought that was a good idea. One of the women she makes up regularly was talking about you with her, and you sounded good to Carol. She gave me your name.

"Carol's expecting you to call her. What are you going to tell her?"

"What do you think I should tell her?"

"Anything except, that you're afraid you may lose her. She won't understand that and she may think it's your way of rejecting her. Just treat her well and don't ask any more from her than you have. How about if I see you next Tuesday. Okay?

"Fine."

Over the weekend, I saw *As Good As It Gets* and as soon as we started on Tuesday, Jerry wanted to talk about it. He didn't pay much attention to the pictures on the walls when he walked in, he really didn't hesitate much at all. He quickly moved the plain chair beside the other chair and sat down. Immediately he said, "You saw the movie? [I nodded] Isn't it spooky? That was me on the screen."

"Jerry, I hope you're not disappointed but it wasn't you. Believe me, there are a lot of Melvins out there avoiding cracks, running locks, and washing their hands. But not many with your back-step walk; it's quite creative. Whether you like it or not, you're not Melvin."

"But the girl, Doc, don't you think Carol's a lot like Karen? She saw something in Melvin, just like Carol sees something in me."

"That part I'll admit is similar. But we never know what happened in the end. You got along great with Carol the first night just like Melvin did with Karen. But when we met last Thursday, you were still getting along well. We don't know what happened between Karen and Melvin. I said to my wife when we walked out of the theater, if he doesn't get some help, my guess is that relationship won't last a week. But forget Melvin. Are you still getting along well with Carol. How did your weekend go?"

"That's what I want to talk to you about; mostly it went well, very well."

"See, that's where I think you may be a lot different from Melvin, you're not as angry as he is. You did say that you have your angry moments, but have you ever tried to harm an animal or to lash out at strangers in a restaurant like he does?"

"No, nothing with animals, I'm even getting to like that cat. But I do have some trouble in restaurants. But not with the customers, it's with the people who seat you. When I have a reservation and they don't honor it I blow up; I'm a big guy, and it can get pretty scary. I did it once with Carol about a week after we met and she had to drag me out of the place. That's one of the reasons I'm seeing you. She didn't say anything but I could see if it happened again. . . . Well, thank goodness, it hasn't happened. But since then I only take her to restaurants where they don't take reservations. But mostly getting seated isn't a problem with Carol. She works days, but almost every night she's out making women up so we don't get out to eat until late. By the way, it was an actress she makes up who gave her the ticket to the Guild that night I met her."

"Could you tell me what you did this weekend? You said it mostly went well; what happened?"

"It was like in the movie, she wanted to go somewhere and I took her. She'd been telling me how much she missed her daughter; she goes to college in Santa Barbara and Carol's too tired to make the drive. I said, 'I'll drive. I'm not tired, you can sleep in the car.' So last Saturday, after she finished with her last client—Saturday's her busiest night—we drove up there. It was late but we were still able to have dinner with her daughter—by the way her name is Jill. But then we did what we'd planned, Carol stayed with Jill in the dorm, her roommate goes home most weekends, and I stayed at a nearby motel. Sunday we had a great day; Jill was thrilled to see her mother so happy with a man. And I turned on what charm I have, and Jill really liked me. I think she also liked the fact that I was more than willing to let her mother stay with her. Like I told you, she and her mother went through a lot with her father. She knows how Carol feels about men and sex and that I respected her feelings. That went a long way with Jill. But it's funny, as comfortable as we were, I just couldn't stifle the urge to wash my hands. During one of the many times I excused myself on Sunday to wash my hands, Carol told Jill about my problem. I didn't like Carol having to do that. Jill looked at me funny for a moment, but at least I kept my silverware in my pocket and I avoided the cracks in a way she didn't notice, so we got through the day. Carol was so happy with me, that helped. . . . Doc, do you think I'll ever get over my craziness?"

"Had Jill seen the movie? Did you bring up the movie?"

"No, it didn't come up."

"I'm glad. Don't bring it up, I don't want her to think of you as Melvin; you're not Melvin; you're not as nasty as he is. And besides, in another way I think you're a lot better off than Melvin."

"What do you mean?"

"You're actually a successful writer, I've seen your name on credits, and once in a while they mention you in the entertainment section. When they made Melvin a writer of romance novels, to me that was a stretch. I couldn't believe a man who writes romance novels would attack people like he did; I mean, even complete strangers. It may have made good cinema but it seemed a bit far fetched to me. Jerry, I know you've got a lot of anger in you. Like when you lashed out at me for not focusing on your craziness when you came into my office on Thursday. But it didn't bother me at all. I knew you were desperate to impress me with how crazy you are. You were trying to get me to pay attention to it. But what you did is very common for people who have symptoms; depressed people do it more than anyone I see. All of you are trying to keep me away from focusing on the real problem, which is always a present relationship. In your case, we don't have to look far for who it is. . . . Would you like to find out why your compulsions are not the real problem? If you're willing to try a little experiment, I can show you."

"Is this going to hurt or anything? What do you mean by an experiment?"

"No, no pain, first an easy question and then a simple request, that's the whole thing. . . . Here's the question. Is that chair, the one you're sitting in, the one most clients sit in?"

"How do I know where your clients sit? Maybe some of them stand."

I disregarded his evasion; he knew the answer.

"Could you choose to get up and move over to the other chair?"

"Why? I like this one."

"Because I asked you to. And if Carol were here, she'd want you to move to that chair, too."

"Carol wouldn't care what chair I was sitting in."

"But she would, Jerry. She'd care very much."

"How do you know that; have you talked to her?"

"You write movies. Think of Carol as one of your heroines. She's fallen for a man who may start to do crazy things or blow up at a moment's notice and then tell her he can't help it. You've been telling her that a lot lately, like you couldn't help it on Sunday when you had to excuse yourself to wash your hands."

"Well, I can't help it. If I could, I wouldn't do what I do."

"Could you choose to move to that chair?"

"What do you mean, 'choose'? Why do you keep saying 'choose'?"

"Because I don't think you're any different from anyone else; we all choose what we do. Maybe not a cough or a sneeze or a twitch, but everything we do that has a purpose, that has some thought behind it. Jerry, you chose to blow up in that restaurant. And now you've chosen to avoid restaurants with reservations because you don't want to take a chance on losing it in front of Carol again. You choose everything you do—the lines, the cracks, the hand washing, the door locks, the picture straightening, the back-stepping, all that crazy stuff."

"I don't choose it. What are you talking about? I'm sick. I've got obsessive-compulsive disease. I can't help myself. Two other doctors have told me that."

This was not a time to get in an argument over the opinions of other doctors. I said, "You chose to put your silverware back into your pocket the first night with Carol at Starbucks; you know you did. While you were sitting there you said to yourself, 'I don't need to do that now in front of her,' and you didn't. Maybe when you went home you back-stepped half the night to relieve the tension of that effort. But if you did, you chose that, too. You can choose to help yourself if you want to—if you can't you're wasting your time with me."

"Okay, I can help myself sometimes but not all the time."

"You can help yourself when you want to."

"But I was with Carol Sunday, and I had to wash my hands. I didn't want to but it felt like I had to."

"You got tense and chose to wash your hands; you didn't have to."

"But why did I get tense? I don't do that anymore with Carol, well hardly anymore. What was the difference yesterday?"

"The only thing I can figure is you were with her daughter, you were trying to impress her, you wanted her to like you. You got nervous and, for years and years, the way you've handled nervousness is with your craziness. Like I said before, it relieves your tension. Exactly why you do it I don't know, but you'd be a lot better off without it. And the first step in getting rid of all the stuff you do is to learn that all your craziness is a choice. If you can learn that, you have a chance to find out a lot more about yourself that I think you need to know to get rid of that stuff."

"I don't believe you. I just flat out don't believe you."

"My God, Jerry, I don't expect you to believe me when I say something this hard for you to accept. But that doesn't mean I'm going to give up. If you're looking for a therapist who gives up, you've come to the wrong one. But how about this? Would you rather it turned out that you were choosing what you do and could learn to make better choices, or would you rather believe you're suffering from a mental illness and you won't ever be able to do anything to help yourself? That maybe your only chance is to take brain drugs? I'm sure the other doctors offered you drugs. I'm surprised you're not on them now. Or maybe you are and haven't told me. That's happened to me a lot."

"I tried a bunch of them. That's why I went to two doctors. But when I was on them I hated how I felt. I'll admit I did do less of my routines, but I couldn't write. Those drugs killed something inside of my brain that I need if I'm to write. I could feel it. It took me a year to get over their effects. I came to you because Carol said she heard you didn't give drugs."

"I'm not dead set against them but I always try talking first, I've either had good clients or I'm lucky, but I've never had to use them. I think you've found out they have a profound effect on your brain, especially, on your creativity. You're a writer, your creativity is all you have. I think you're right to be careful; I've heard a few stories like your's. . . . But c'mon, we're wasting time: Can you choose to move to that chair?"

He looked at me in desperation, I was asking a lot more of him than to move to another chair. I was asking him to choose to give up a way of life that he'd been choosing for years, maybe since he was a teenager. A life like Melvin Udall's is not built in a day. I have to go by my feelings, and I felt that we'd connected enough so that asking him to move to a chair with a pattern on it was worth a try. He did get what I was driving at. He said, "It's important that I move, isn't it?"

"If it weren't I wouldn't have asked you to."

"But I don't want to move to that chair. Why should I move for you? I hardly know you."

"Jerry, do you trust anyone?"

A long pause and then,

"I think I can trust Carol. And before you started giving me that 'move to that chair' crap, I thought I could trust you."

"So if you're to trust me, I've got to go along with your belief that you're mentally ill. That you can't help what you're doing?"

"Yes, goddamn it, I am mentally ill, and all you're doing to help me is ask me to change chairs. What kind of help is that?"

I felt for him, for his frustration. All I was asking him to do was change the way he'd been living his life for maybe forty years. I'd begun to make my point. There was no need to push farther.

"It's not important to me where you sit. But I think it's very important that you trust me enough to think seriously about making the move."

"What do you mean, trust you? How can I trust you? I'm paying you to help me. How can you trust anyone you have to pay to talk to?"

"I'm trusting you to pay me. Am I making a mistake?"

"No, damn it, it's not a mistake; you'll get your dough. In cash as soon as we finish."

"So I can trust you. That's enough for me. As long as I can trust you, we won't have any problem."

It's going to take a little more time, but I believe he's beginning to trust me. I wouldn't be surprised to see him sit in the regular chair the next time he comes in.

"But why am I this way? What's wrong with me? Was it my childhood? I didn't think it was so bad."

"Jerry, I don't have to hear about your childhood; it may have had an effect on you, but it's long gone. Your problem is now. You're lonely and you need someone. Carol may be that someone. You certainly hope she is. But you're afraid you're going to lose her. That's why you're here, and that's what I'm trying to help you with. And we're making progress, but my way is not to go back, the problem is now, not in your past. We can go back through your whole life and make all kinds of guesses about why things happened, but what for? Nothing that's ever happened to you is preventing you from moving to that chair. And nothing that's ever happened to you is stopping you from trusting me. And nothing that's ever happened to you is going to stop you from loving Carol if you keep getting along with her as well as you are now. You know something's seriously wrong with your life. You've known it for years, but now you're trying to do something about it."

"You really think you can help me, don't you?"

"Yes. I really think I can help you. But you've got to help, too. You've got to do something for yourself, something you've never thought of doing, something no one has ever asked you to do."

"Doc, I don't want to lose her. I'll try to do anything you suggest."

He trusts me. It may take a while, but I think I'll be able to help him.

"Jerry, you've been choosing your compulsions a long time. It's not going to be easy to stop making those choices. And I don't want you to try to force yourself to stop. Doing what Carol did on Sunday, telling Jill about your problem, was the right thing to do. If you'd tried to force yourself to stop, you wouldn't have been able to, things would have gotten worse, and you might have ruined your whole weekend. Between now and when I see you again next week, do your things, it's okay. But whenever you do, say to yourself, *Jerry, I'm choosing to do this, whatever it may be*. Try to understand it's a choice. That's all. Will you try?"

He nodded.

"Can you come again next Tuesday? If you can't wait that long, call me and I'll see you. Or if you just want to talk for a few minutes, call me. And be sure to tell Carol what we talked about. Ask her that if she sees you do any of your 'things' to remind you that they're choices. That's all, just remind you. If it's all right with you, I'll see you next week at this same time."

Before he left, he paid me in cash for the two visits. Later in the book, I'll revisit Jerry.

2

Reality Therapy in Action Is Supported by Choice Theory

As long as clients continue to use the choice theory they've learned in the counseling, the therapy never ends.

For you to understand better the reality therapy I use with every client in this book, I would like to pause here to explain a little more about choice theory. Reality therapy, based on choice theory, is a unique counseling method. For example:

1. I believe people choose the behavior that has led them into therapy because it is always their best effort to deal with a present, unsatisfying relationship—or, worse, no relationships at all.
2. The task of the counselor is to help clients choose new relationship-improving behaviors that are much closer to satisfying one or more of their five basic needs than the ones they are presently choosing. This means improving their ability to find more *love and belonging, power, freedom,* and *fun*. *Survival* is also a basic need, and some people come for counseling when their lives are in danger.
3. To satisfy every need, we must have good relationships with other people. This means that satisfying the need for

love and belonging is the key to satisfying the other four needs.

4. Because love and belonging, like all the needs, can be satisfied only in the present, reality therapy focuses almost exclusively on the here and now.
5. Although many of us have been traumatized in the past, we are not the victims of our past unless we presently choose to be. The solution to our problem is rarely found in explorations of the past unless the focus is on past successes.
6. The pain or the symptoms that clients choose is not important to the counseling process. We may never find out why one lonely person may choose to depress, another to obsess, a third to crazy, and a fourth to drink. In fact, if we focus on the symptom, we enable the client to avoid the real problem, which is improving present relationships.
7. The continuing goal of reality therapy is to create a choice-theory relationship between the client and the counselor. By experiencing this satisfying relationship, clients can learn a lot about how to improve the troubled relationship that brought them into counseling.
8. To understand why the seven points just mentioned are integral to practicing reality therapy, it is helpful if clients read the 1998 book, *Choice Theory: A New Psychology of Personal Freedom,* and the 1999 book, *The Language of Choice Theory*. If clients can't or won't read these books, the therapist can teach them the choice theory they need to know as the counseling proceeds.

Although there are many misconceptions about therapy in general, most people believe it is slow and costs a lot of money. This is not true of reality therapy. In many instances, much can be accomplished in one session, and ten to twelve sessions are often sufficient. If the client is willing to read the two earlier books I listed, the time for therapy can be substantially shortened.

Besides the availability of the books, what makes reality therapy so efficient is that we do not spend much time in the past, except to look for past strengths; we listen to, but do not focus on, the pain or symptom; and reality therapy gets quickly to the actual problem—improving a present relationship or finding a new, more satisfying one.

The length of the therapy is related more to how quickly the therapist can create a good client-therapist relationship based on choice theory than to anything else. The sooner this relationship is created, the less time will be needed for therapy. If therapists cannot create such a relationship, therapy will almost always fail. When using reality therapy, we do not pursue the following traditional strategies:

1. Dreams need not be explored or even mentioned. Time spent on dreams is time wasted.

2. Clients should not be labeled with a diagnosis except when necessary for insurance purposes. From our standpoint, diagnoses are descriptions of the behaviors people choose to deal with the pain and frustration that is endemic to unsatisfying present relationships.

3. We believe that the current accepted concept that clients are the victims of mental illness caused by a neurochemical imbalance *over which they have no control* is wrong. If it was true, no psychotherapy could be effective. The so-called neurochemical imbalance that is cited as the major causes of mental illness is a myth. The brain is not defective. Its chemistry is normal for the behaviors clients choose (see Chapter Four of *Choice Theory*). Brain drugs, such as Prozac, may make clients feel better but cannot teach them how to connect or reconnect with people they need.

4. What I call mental illness are conditions, such as Alzheimer's disease, epilepsy, head trauma, and brain infections, as well as genetic defects, such as Down's syndrome, Huntington's chorea, and autism. People with these conditions are suffering from brain abnormalities and should be treated primarily by neurologists. Although they may not be candidates for reality therapy, most will benefit from a relationship with a warm, supportive person.

The whole purpose of this book is to take you into my office as I counsel so you can clearly see what I do. I also suggest that you read *Choice Theory* and compare the theory in that book with any other theory you may know. When you do so, you will easily be able to appreciate the theoretical and practical differences between what I and others do. These differences do not mean that reality therapy is better than other therapies; that is for both readers and clients to decide.

An important difference between reality therapy and other therapies is that we teach choice theory to clients as part of their therapy. In this book I make an effort to show how we do so. Feedback from many people who have read *Choice Theory* has led me to believe that many people who read this book have learned to live their lives in a way that maintains and improves relationships. In much of counseling, when the actual visits with the counselor are over, the therapy is over. As long as clients continue to use the choice theory they've learned in reality therapy, the therapy never ends.

Finally, on a semantic note, if our behaviors are chosen, it is inaccurate to describe them by using nouns and adjectives. To be accurate, verbs are the only part of speech that should be used to describe behavior. For example, the commonly used terms *depression* (a noun) or *depressed* (an adjective) are inaccurate. Following choice theory, we would use the verb forms *depressing* (a gerund) or *choosing to depress* (an infinitive).

But using verbs is much more important than just using

correct grammar. It follows logically that if we *choose to depress,* we can also *choose to stop depressing.* Using verbs points us in the direction of choosing more effective behaviors. When we use nouns and adjectives (for example, *depression* and *depressed*) to describe our choice to depress, as most people and almost all therapists do, we tend to avoid the real problem: that what we are complaining about is *a choice.*

It is obvious that Jerry, like Melvin Udall in *As Good As It Gets,* is choosing what he does, and in the therapy he will begin to make better choices. In the first paragraph of the first chapter, you may have noticed that I used verbs, such as *to obsess* and *compulse* to describe his behavior. As you read further, you will see many examples of this usage, and after a while, I believe it will make sense to you.

For example, the next time you are a little "depressed," don't say to yourself or to anyone else: "I'm depressed." Instead, say, "I'm choosing to depress because a relationship in my life is not working for me right now. I'm going to try to figure out a better choice." If you take this suggestion, you will immediately begin to see how correct grammar may lead you to conclude, *If I choose all I do, maybe I can choose to do something better.*

3

LUCY

We all want a perfect world populated by perfect people like us, but that world has never existed.

Lucy was a voluntary client who was a little early for her first appointment. I'll work with her as I do with all clients by going as far and as fast as possible in the first session. Therapy time is precious. I want her to leave this first session believing she had some help. In most of the client-therapist exchanges written in this book, I omit the chit-chat that occurs in all therapy and focus on the part that leads the client to consider choosing to change.

When Lucy walked in the door, I greeted her with a handshake and observed that she was a well-dressed, attractive woman who appeared to be about fifty years old. She was of average weight and height and looked healthy but not happy; she almost had to force a smile when she came in. She was wearing a wedding ring, so I assumed she was either married or widowed.

I took her name and address; I already had her phone number from when she made the appointment. I did not discuss finances. I assume I will be paid, and I think that tackling the subject of fees immediately is counterproductive to establishing the relationship with clients that is so important. If I can help her in the first session, which I believe I will be able to do, I will get paid. I will work with her, as with all clients, to find a fee she can afford.

As in the previous chapter, I will stop whenever it seems necessary to explain what I am thinking as the therapy progresses. I started, as I almost always do with a voluntary client, by saying,

"Lucy, you came here for a good reason. It would help me a lot if you'd start by telling me what's on your mind?"

I don't ask her what her problem is or lead her in any direction. It's just an open-ended question that assumes she has something on her mind that brought her to see me. I know that she, like all clients, is struggling with an unsatisfying relationship and that she is in some pain because of this struggle. I always wonder, will she bring up the relationship or will I have to ask?

"I'm miserable. It's been going on a long time, over five years, and it doesn't seem to be getting any better. Mostly I'm depressed, but lately I've been getting these rages. I mean, I want to throw things, break something. I can fly off the handle anytime and with anybody. Yesterday my mother called and asked how I was feeling, and I blew up. I yelled and cursed and told her it was none of her goddamn business. She knows I've been upset, she didn't mean any harm, and I went crazy. It can happen at the store when I'm shopping; with my grown kids when they phone; and, more and more, it's been happening with my husband. The only place I'm comfortable is in school; I'm a middle school English teacher. That's the good part of my life. The rest is a nightmare. I'm either way down or in a rage. Recently, I've been getting these splitting headaches on weekends. I can't go on like this. I heard about you, and I need help."

There's obviously something very wrong. This is a lot to get from a first question. My initial guess is that she's in a huge conflict. She's thrashing around, depressing, raging, headaching. It shouldn't be too hard to find out what relationship has gone sour. I'll focus; I'm sure she's ready to tell me.

"We can save a lot of time if you'll tell me what's really wrong. My experience tells me that there's an important relationship that's not working for you right now. I'd like to know who it is and what's wrong."

"Who it is and what's wrong? I just walk in the door, and you ask me that. How do I know if I can trust you? I don't even know you. Maybe I don't want to answer that question."

"Oh no. You want to answer that question. That question's on your mind all the time. But you're right, you don't know if you can trust me. It also shouldn't be too hard for you to figure out that if you can't trust me, I can't help you. Maybe we should start by talking about trust because it's obviously on your mind. Maybe that'll help you."

Now she's let the cat a little out of the bag. It seems that whatever's gone wrong in the relationship has to do with trust. At her age, it's most likely something with her husband. And her depressing is no longer keeping the anger in check. She's blowing up at everyone. She wants people to know how angry she is. She's also screaming for help, but she's so angry she's irrational and putting all her relationships in jeopardy. She's held off on her husband for a while, she needs him more than the others, but now she's letting him have it, too. But maybe all this anger is a good sign. She wants to come to grips with the problem instead of denying it by choosing to depress, rage, headache, or somaticize.

"I'm acting stupid, aren't I? I have to trust you, don't I?"

"You really do. But go slow. Question everything I say. Ask me to explain myself. If you can understand where I'm coming from, I don't think you have to worry about me hurting you. There's nothing hidden on my part. I'm ready to give you a reason for everything I say."

That seemed to reassure her. I can see her relax. And it's the way I like to do therapy. Clue the client in on all my thinking. Let her point out what she doesn't understand. This way, we can build an honest relationship. That kind of relationship is obviously missing in her life right now.

"Okay, I'll tell you what's wrong. It's my husband. It's a story that I'm sure you've heard a million times, but this one's a little different. It turns out he works for a woman. She's the boss. They used to travel a lot together and they had an affair. It lasted three years. I found out she's been doing this for years. He isn't the first one. Two other wives told me about it; they'd suffered through the same thing, and their husbands told them what had happened. And they felt it was their duty to tell me. With that woman, it's one man at a time. I'd heard rumors about the way she was, but I didn't think it would be that way with my husband. I guess you never think that. Anyway, it's over now. She's on to someone else, and my husband has a different job in the company and doesn't travel with her anymore. But here's the point: I can't get over it. I just can't accept what he did; I can't trust him anymore. He has opportunities; maybe he's involved with someone else. It's destroying my life because I still love him. When he tries to be good to me, it really pisses me off and I blow up. I'm fifty-two years old. I don't want a divorce; I don't want to start over. But I can't seem to forgive him. I'm a basket case. What can you do for me?"

"Has your husband admitted it?"

"No, he denies everything. I've confronted him, but he won't admit anything. He says he knew that the other men went to bed with her, but he didn't. He says he doesn't even like her. He says he loves me. That I should trust him. That I'm driving myself crazy over nothing. But I don't believe him. I hate the fact that he keeps lying. To tell you the truth, I think I'd feel better if he admitted it. That, at least, would be honest."

"If he hasn't admitted it after all this time, I doubt if he will. What good would it do now anyway?"

"What good would it do? It'd be honest. I can't stand living with a liar."

"I don't think that right now it makes any difference whether he did or didn't do it."

"How can you say that? It makes all the difference in the world? And he did do it; I know he did."

"Lucy, that's what I'm trying to tell you. Right now you *know* he did it. It doesn't make any difference what he says. You've put him on trial and found him guilty. I'm not saying you're wrong to think this way. All I'm saying is this is where you are, today, right now. No matter how depressed you choose to be, how much you choose to rage or headache, it won't change anything he's done or not done. In your mind he's guilty, and he can't do a thing about it. Lucy, can you tell me what you really want right now?"

"What do you mean I choose to be depressed? What are you talking about? I don't want to feel this way. It's what he did that's *making* me feel this way."

I've introduced a little choice theory and she's rejecting it in favor of external control by blaming him. But I've sewn the only seed that can help her—that all she can control is her own behavior, that whatever she does, it's her choice. I've got to nurture that seed because as long as she chooses to feel miserable over what she's convinced he did, no one can help her. Whether he did or didn't do it is not the point. She may never find out what he actually did. But she says she loves him and wants to stay married to him. If she didn't, she wouldn't choose to be so upset. I've got to help her figure out how to accept him again. If she can't, whether they divorce or not, she may be dooming herself to a life of misery. She's caught in the conflict between wanting to love and not willing to trust, and only she can resolve it. But I can help.

"It will help if you'll answer the question I just asked. Please try."

"What question? You said I'm choosing to feel the way I'm feeling. That's not a question. That's crazy."

"I'm sorry. I guess when I said that thing about choosing, that's all you heard. The question I actually asked was, What do you want right now?"

"Oh, that's easy. I want to trust my husband. I want a good marriage like the one I thought I had."

"But I guess you're too angry to trust."

"Angry is putting it mildly. I'm furious."

Okay, that takes care of some of the problem; she admits her choice to continue to anger is keeping her misery going. And she said she wants to trust him and wants to keep her marriage; that's positive. I'll ask her another question that may help her shift to the present, rather than continue to be stuck in the past.

"How about this question: If you could have a wish, what would you wish right now?"

"That's easy. That wish is on my mind all the time. I wish it'd never happened. I wish he'd never met that woman. I wish I weren't sitting here telling you this. I wish I weren't depressed and full of rage. And right now, I seem to be getting a headache, and I wish it'd go away. If you want to talk about wishes, I'm full of wishes."

Now I've gotten her to the point where she may be able to realize she is faced with an impossibility. It'll take some time, but I've got to teach her that none of us can wish the past away. That all any of us can control is our own present behavior. We all want a perfect world populated by perfect people like us, but that world has never existed. If it did, there would be no need for psychotherapy. As you can see, I'm not going to get into whether it happened or not; only her husband knows that. To do so would be to muddy the water even more. I'm going to get into what she can do now whether he's guilty or innocent. That's the issue I'm going to try to get her to face.

"I wish it hadn't happened either. I'm fairly sure your husband wishes it hadn't happened if he's guilty, and I'm totally sure he wishes you'd stop accusing him if he's not guilty. You're not the only one with wishes here."

I think that bringing up the idea that he has some wishes, too, will change the focus, maybe help her see there is another side of the story, his side. All she's thinking about right now is herself. And she's stuck. She's like a piece of paper on a sharp spindle. She can turn and twist, but she can't wish herself off. Let's see what she says to my reference to her husband.

"So what are you saying? I should just forget about it? Don't you think I've tried?"

"I'm sure you've tried. But you've tried all by yourself. You haven't included him at all. Are you aware of what you just said?"

"What did I just say?"

"Well, I heard you say, 'I should just forget about it.' And that you've tried."

"Well, I have. There have even been times when I've come close, but I can't."

"No, that's not right. So far you haven't been willing to forget. And you don't know what you can do later on; there's no sense trying to guess about that. You only know what you can or can't do now. But you also told me, 'I can't go on like this!' What do you mean by that?"

"Well, I can't; I'm miserable. If I didn't love him, I'd be okay. I don't want a divorce."

"If you wanted a divorce, you wouldn't have come to see me. But what's going on can change. It doesn't have to keep happening unless you choose to keep it happening. Things in a relationship are always changing. We're doing something right now you've never done before. You're talking the situation over rationally with someone you're trying to trust. That makes a big difference."

"I'm so upset and mixed up I don't know what I want. And you're confusing me with all this crap about choosing."

"I'm not confusing you. You know exactly what you want; you told me. Could I be telling you what you've been wanting to hear?"

"That it's okay to forget what happened?"

"Lucy, it's not a perfect world. You didn't marry a perfect man, but you love him. And you're not a perfect woman. You've made your point. Five years is enough. . . . Tell me, what did you do last night?"

While she thinks about letting it go, I'll shift gears with my last question. It's a technique I've used for years. Be specific and avoid general questions; generalities are too easy to hold onto. What happened last night will tell me the present state of her marriage as clearly as anything else, and then let's see how many more nights like this she wants.

"There was nothing unusual about last night, if that's what you're driving at. We ate dinner, he watched television for a while, I graded papers. Then we went to bed. We didn't talk much; I was my usual depressed self. I didn't even feel angry last night."

"How many more nights like this do you want?"

This question is again specific. It looks as if she's losing her anger. This is not a good sign. There's a sense of resignation that concerns me. The good part is that it's obvious she's sick and tired of what's been going on.

"What do you expect me to say? I don't trust him anymore. We get along, but not much more. He's accepted that this is the way I am."

"Sex?"

"When he wants it. Not very often. I don't initiate anything, if that's what you're driving at. Our bodies still touch at night; we haven't stopped wanting to feel the other's there. I guess if we stopped that, the marriage'd really be over.

"Was there any rage last night, did you feel any anger?"

"It's there, it's always right beneath the surface."

That's a good sign. She's hasn't given up.

"Is the anger directed at him?"

"I guess so, but I'm not a violent person. It's directed more at things. Like lately I've been getting the feeling I'd like to smash the television. It used to be dishes; I'd like to hear something crash."

All I can think of is that she wants something to happen. But if she smashes the television, that would make things worse. Violence never solves problems. It's time to step in and make a direct suggestion. If she rejects it, I'll back off but do it in a way that keeps it in front of her.

"Okay, I've asked a lot of questions, and I've found out a

lot about you. You just said you'd like to hear something crash. So would I. What could you do that would make a big crash in your life? I'm thinking of a positive crash, I'm not thinking about smashing the TV."

"A positive crash? I don't know what you mean."

"How about telling your husband, 'I love you. The past is over. Whatever you did or didn't do, I can't do a thing about it. I've been trying to fix the past for years, and I can't do it.' Because Lucy, you have been trying to fix it, and you haven't succeeded. And you'll never succeed. You know it; you've known it for a long time. Put the past in an imaginary bottle and throw it out the window. Let it smash into a million pieces."

"But what do I do with all my feelings."

"Put them in the bottle with the past. It'll take a while, but you can do it. You're looking for a way out. You wouldn't have come here if you weren't."

"What if he rejects me? I've given him a real hard time."

"What if he doesn't? Could that be what you're worried about?"

"You mean to just stop what I've been doing?"

"Stop what you've been choosing to do. It's enough already; it's been five years; you've made your point. Let it go. If you've been trying to punish him, you've succeeded. If you were trying to punish yourself, you've done a great job."

"What if he asks me what happened, why I've changed?"

"Tell him the truth. Tell him you came to see me. Ask him to come in with you the next time. I'd like to see both of you for an hour."

"But, is this it? Everyone says therapy takes years."

"It's not over. But we're off to a good start. It's going to be hard to let what happened go. If you could bring your husband in, I think I could help both of you. But let me warn you. If he comes in, I'm not going to talk about what happened or didn't happen. I only want to talk about right now and the immediate future. Is that okay?"

"I'm sick of the past. But letting it go is a little scary."

"Letting anything go that you've been holding onto for a long time is scary. There's a strong part of you that says, *It's not the thing to do; he has no right to expect me to forgive him*. That's why we still have a way to go. Call me if you want to talk, and I'll see you at the same time next week."

When clients are trying to make big changes in their lives, I always make myself available. They don't abuse the privilege. But if Lucy could persuade her husband to come in, I'd very much like to work with them both. But that wasn't to be. She called me the next day to say that her husband flatly refused to come in with her or without her. He told her that it was bad enough hearing it from her, he didn't want some doctor ganging up on him, too. Besides, he said he didn't need a shrink; he needed her to stop accusing him of something he didn't do.

I continued to see her, but I just kept repeating this session, asking her in a variety of ways: *How long do you want to choose to be miserable?* It took six more once-a-week sessions until she saw that if she didn't give up her accusations, her marriage would be over. It was already in bad shape. As far as I was concerned, we really didn't accomplish that much in the next six sessions, but they were needed to keep reminding her to let the past go. It takes time for people like Lucy, who mire themselves in external control, to extricate themselves from it. During this time, I gave her *Choice Theory* to read, and reading that book helped her.

4

Bea and Jim

What kind of a counselor are you? I don't think you know what you're doing. You don't ask how I feel; you don't want to hear about my suffering. What are we doing here, anyway?

In contrast to Lucy, whose husband refused to come with her, Bea and Jim, who had a similar problem, came together for help. Like Lucy, Bea was very angry, but she had something more tangible to be angry about: Jim admitted to having an affair. What I want to show is how I counsel a married couple *no matter what the problem*. I would have done the same if Lucy's husband had been willing to come in.

When a couple comes for counseling, I use a method of marital counseling I developed, called *structured reality therapy.* This method emphasizes that marriage is a partnership and that the only way to help a troubled couple like Bea and Jim is to focus on what's *good for their marriage,* not on what may be good for one or the other.

Because this counseling has a rigid structure, it surprises most couples. They expect me to be more sympathetic, especially to the partner who believes he or she is the victim. There is a purpose to not getting involved in a discussion of how each partner feels because, in my experience, such a discussion leads the counseling astray. By being given a chance to express a great deal of misery, each partner will inevitably try to draw the counselor into taking sides. Any marriage counselor who even intimates that one partner is more responsible than the other for the problem, risks doing further harm to the marriage.

This way to counsel couples may seem, at first glance, simplistic, but if you are a marriage counselor, I urge you to try it. You will find that couples understand it and know how to use it by the end of the second session. Quickly, it leads couples away from the external control that is wrecking their marriage to the choice theory that can save it. What goes on in this highly structured approach will become clear as I counsel Bea and Jim.

Bea and Jim were in their early forties, and nothing about their looks or background was unusual. I will not describe them; rather, picture them yourself. We all know a couple in their early forties who are unhappily married. Think of that couple as I counsel, it will make what I do more personal.

After the usual getting-acquainted amenities, I started by saying, "The way this works is I'm going to ask you five questions. For the counseling to be effective, it is important that each of you answer each question in your own way. Please try not to talk at the same time. The questions will not be difficult, but I have to have a satisfactory answer to all of them from each of you. I'm not going to play games. I am more than willing to explain why I think an answer is not acceptable. I'll try not to be harsh, but if I am, it's because I want to make sure you understand how important it is that you stick to answering the questions."

Doc: Are you here, Bea, are you here, Jim, because you want help for your marriage? I mean you're not here because you want a divorce but are seeing me first because you don't want to feel guilty about breaking up the marriage. Okay, who wants to start?"

Jim: I want help; this marriage is a disaster. I hate living with her like this. I love her, but there doesn't seem to be anything I can do to satisfy her.

Bea: I'm here because of him. I feel betrayed; I can't get over the feeling.

Doc: Please, Bea, I understand how you feel, and I'm sure Jim knows how you feel. It's a simple question; just answer it. Do you want help with your marriage, or is this, for you, a prelude to a divorce?

Bea: Of course, I want help. I don't want a divorce. I told you that last week when I made the appointment.

Doc: But please be more clear. Do you want help personally or for your marriage? That's still the question I want you to answer.

Bea: If that's what I need to get a better marriage, I want both. If my marriage gets better, I'll feel better, too.

Doc: Okay, that's fine. Here's the next question: Whose behavior can you control? Jim?

Jim: That's easy; I sure can't control hers.

Doc: I'm sorry to be so picky, but that's not what I asked you. I didn't ask whose behavior you can't control; I asked, whose you can.

Bea: If I could control him, I wouldn't be here. I can't; that's why I'm here.

Doc: Look, please, it's a simple question; just answer it. Whose behavior can each of you control?

Bea: Okay, I can see what you're driving at. I can control mine. . . . A lot of good that does me living with him.

Jim: Mine; I can only really control mine.

You can see how each of them is almost totally focused on the other as the source of the problem. Since choice theory states that the only person's behavior we can control is our own, I have to nudge them toward that realization. That's why I'm being so particular. Any marital counseling that allows one partner to blame the other will harm the marriage. I'll be as polite as I can be, but I have to be firm here. The next question does allow them a brief opportunity to blame the other. But it's a necessary step so they can later see the difference it has made in their marriage when they give up external control for choice theory.

Doc: Fine, you're getting the idea. You can only control what you do, not what anyone else does. This next question will give you a chance to express your feelings. There's no hurry. Okay, here's the third question: Would each of you tell me what you believe is wrong with the marriage right now?

Bea: Him, I told you the story; he had an affair, and I can't deal with it. He doesn't deny it, but he won't talk about it. He says it's over. But how do I know it's over? Since I found out what he did, I don't believe anything he says. To me it's like the bottom's dropped out of the marriage. I want him to talk about it, not just admit it and say it's over. If he'd do that, then maybe I could get over it. At least it wouldn't seem as if I'm living with someone who doesn't care how I feel.

Jim: How do you think I feel? I didn't deny it; it happened a few times, and it's over. Why rehash the details? They weren't even gory. She thinks I'm covering up a lot more. I've told her the truth, but she isn't satisfied. Tell me Doctor, how in the world could anyone deal with that?

Doc: Anything else? Is that the whole thing?

Jim: I can't say we've had a perfect marriage, but it was pretty good. No matter what I did, I never stopped loving her. Now it's all changed. I'll tell you, Doctor, I'm never going to say any more than I just said. But if she wants, I'll repeat it over and over.

Bea: You see, that's what's wrong. He did something wrong, and he won't talk to me about it. I want to know who; I want to know when and where. Where is that woman? I want her phone number; I may want to talk to her. Since he won't talk, I'd like to hear her side of the story. It's not enough for me that it's over. It's not over in my head. I don't trust him. I can't live with him the way he is.

Here you can clearly see how each of them is making a case for me to take sides. As long as I maintain the structure, they will not be able to do so. After Bea's last speech, Jim just listened with a look of resignation on his face. He didn't say anything in rebuttal.

Doc: All right, I think you've both answered question number three satisfactorily. Are you ready for the next question?

Bea: What do you mean, we both answered the question satisfactorily? You're a man. To a man, a total cover-up is satisfactory. What kind of a counselor are you? I don't think you know what you're doing. You don't ask how I feel; you don't want to hear about my suffering. What are we doing here, anyway?

This is another attempt by Bea to try to force me into taking her side. I don't side with either of them. If I did, the other would become even more resentful, which is exactly what I am trying to avoid. I don't take sides, but I do take *a* side. I'm on the side of the marriage.

Jim: You see what I have to put up with. You've heard her ranting and raving for a few minutes. I have to live with it day and night. The affair is over. If she wants to check up on me, she can. I'll help; I'll give her my schedule, call in, anything she wants, but I won't talk to her about it anymore than I have. Maybe she's so insistent because she's covering up for something she did; things like that happen.

Bea: You son-of-a-bitch, you know I've always been 100 percent faithful to you.

Jim: How do I know that?

Bea: Because I'm telling you. Have you ever had any reason to doubt me?

Doc: Look, you're both unhappy. I'm trying to help. You've answered the questions fine so far. Let's go on. It doesn't make any sense to fight here. Things are bad enough. Why make them worse?

After I said that, I paused and looked at them trying to send the message that we'd all be better off if they listen carefully to what I'm asking them to do.

Doc: I'm trying to help your marriage—that's what you came here for.

Even with all the disagreement, I think they're beginning to get the point: Their marriage is more important than what each of them thinks is right.

Doc: OK, you've both convinced me that there's a lot wrong with your marriage. I think we ought to go on to the fourth question. Tell me, in your opinion, what's good about your marriage right now? Take your time, but please focus on what's good. I'd like to warn you ahead of time that if either one of you believes that there's nothing good about your marriage, then the counseling is over, and there's no charge. You pay only if the counseling works.

There was a long pause. Bea and Jim looked puzzled and somewhat skeptical. This was a totally unexpected question. Neither of them had thought about what was good in the marriage for a long time, maybe not since their honeymoon. To reassure them, I said:

Doc: Take your time. Think about it.

Jim: Well . . . she's a good mother. She keeps a good house. She doesn't spend too much money. . . . And she used to be a lot of fun.

Doc: I hate to nitpick, Jim, but I didn't ask what she used to be. Is she any fun now?

Jim: It's still there. But as soon as she starts to have fun, she catches herself as if she's doing something wrong. Oh, I forgot. She's a good cook; no that's not right, she's a great cook. She hasn't closed down that part of the marriage.

Bea: I haven't closed down any part of the marriage. How could I enjoy sex with you anymore? Sure, it used to be fun but not anymore. I talked with my minister, and he told me not to turn the sex off, so I haven't.

Doc: Please, Bea. There must be something good left in your marriage. If there isn't, I can't help you.

Bea: I'm not asking you to help me. I'm asking you to help him. How can we have a marriage if he's all closed up? My God, Jim, you don't even apologize.

Jim: Look, I'm willing to admit I was wrong; it's all my fault. I'm not blaming you at all. You've always been a good wife, and you didn't deserve this. But that's all I'm going to say. The more I tell you, the more you want to hear. You want to make a big deal about something that happened three years ago that has very little to do with our lives now. I'm not going to give you the name of the woman. She's married; she doesn't need you calling her or her husband. If we keep talking about it, you'll rehash it for the next fifty years. Remember the doctor's question, *Whose behavior can you control?* Well, I can't control your behavior, and you can't control mine. I can see why the doctor asked that question.

Doc: Bea, please tell me what's good. I want to help you, but I have to hear from you that there's something good left in this marriage.

Jim: Tell him, Bea. Please. Let's get some help; answer his question.

Bea: Okay. He's a good provider. We bank my salary for the kids' college. He's a good father, and, until the last three years, he's always been a very easy man to live with. I talk to my friends. They tell me how difficult their husbands are. Jim was never like that until this trouble started. How's that? Is that a good enough answer for you?

Doc: Thank you. I appreciate both your answers. It'll really help me in what I'm trying to do. Now we're ready to go on to the last question. This question's different from the others in the sense that it's less important that you try to figure out what I want. It's more important that you please each other. . . . Each of you tell me what's one thing that you, Bea, and you, Jim, could do all this coming week that you think will make your marriage better? Assuming that each of you can come up with something, then you'll go home and do it for a week. If you don't do it, or if it doesn't help the marriage, then I don't see any sense in you coming back. But let's not worry about that right now. Let's see what you each come up with.

I say this to make sure they know how important this question is. That the success of the counseling is riding on their ability to do what they are now going to tell each other.

Bea: You mean this could be the last session if we can't answer that question? I've been suffering with this guy for three years. We need more time to work it out. Jim, don't you agree?

This is a good sign. She's turning to him for help against me. This is the payoff for me not taking sides. The goal is for them to align themselves with each other, not with me against the other.

Jim: Bea, the doctor is not throwing us out. And I think I'm beginning to catch on to what he's trying to do. I think we'd be better off if we do what he says. I'm going along with him. I'd like it if you would, too.

Doc: Bea, believe me, I know what I'm doing. If you can do what I hope you're going to suggest, then the next session could provide you with lifetime marriage counseling. I think it's worth a try, or I wouldn't ask you to do it.

Bea: Okay, big shot. You say you know what the doctor's doing. So tell me, what are you going to do all next week that'll make the marriage better?

Jim: I don't want to go first. You go first. You're the one who's wrecking the marriage by all your anger. I want to hear what you'll do. Then I'll try to improve on whatever it is.

Bea: OK, I could cook you a good dinner every night—all the things you like.

Doc: I'm not saying good dinners are not important, but I'm looking for something more than that. Something personal—something you do with each other.

Jim: Wait a minute, I just got a good idea. It's summer. You've got a week coming. I've been working a lot of overtime lately; I can take a week off. I say let's get in the car, drop the kids off in San Luis Obispo at my folks, and then go on to San Francisco for a week. We can afford it. We haven't spent a dime on recreation for so long I can't remember. We used to love San Francisco; let's go.

Bea: But what does that change? So we have a good week, so what?

Doc: But listen to what you just said, "So we have a good week." Tell me, when was the last time you had a good week? Do you think a good week with Jim would help your marriage?

Jim: I don't want to sound selfish, but it'd sure help mine.

After a long pause:

Bea: Okay, I'll go . . . and I'll not mention a word about that woman for a whole week. . . . I really love the idea of going to San Francisco.

Doc: Come back to see me as soon as you get home; it doesn't have to be exactly a week. Call me.

It's possible I'll be criticized for the counseling I just did. People will say it's too simple; no angry woman would give up her anger so easily. I believe the opposite: The more a counselor talks about her anger, the harder it is for her to let it go. What Bea wants from Jim is impossible. She may be curious about what the other woman has that she doesn't have, but for whatever reason, she's trying to make him talk about the affair, and he won't do it. As much as she would like, she can't make him do something he doesn't want to do. No counseling can change that reality. What happened, happened. They can talk about it for all eternity; it will never change.

My experience is that each person in an unhappy marriage may be quite competent outside the marriage. But outside the marriage, it's easier to be competent; external control still exists but not to the extent it does in marriage. It is the constant trying to force the other to be different or to punish each other for real or perceived wrongs that causes almost all the problems. Apologies work to some extent, but if the aggrieved party wants more, as Bea evidently does, they are worthless.

You can't build anything therapeutic on misery and anger. But if they go to San Francisco and have a good time, there's a lot that can be done as soon as they come back. If they don't have a good week, I'll offer to repeat what I did or to give up. I have no alternatives to this approach. But my initial threat to give up has put a little pressure on them; they don't want me to give up because they don't want to give up, or they wouldn't have come in the first place.

Actually, the only questions most couples have trouble with are the last two. If they can't answer question four, I don't think there's much hope for the marriage. If they can't give a good answer to question five and then go ahead and do it, I begin to have doubts. But depending on how I appraise the situation, I may work with them further in the hopes that they will eventually work out what to do with each other that will help the marriage. If they refuse to answer any question or refuse to do what they said they would do in question five, I tell them that I believe they don't really want help. If they then look around for someone to blame, I tell them they can blame themselves. The real strength of structured reality therapy marriage counseling is that this whole process is so clear and straightforward.

As most couples do, they followed through and went to San Francisco. I really didn't have to ask how it went, I could see it on their faces when they came in. But asking was a way to get the process started:

Doc: I guess you went to San Francisco. How'd it go?

Bea: We had a marvelous time. If that woman was still on his mind, we couldn't have had a week like that. We saw shows, visited museums, and strolled through Golden Gate Park. I needed that week.

Jim: It's like Bea said, if we didn't have a good marriage, we couldn't have had such a good time. When we checked out of the St. Francis, we made a reservation to come back for our anniversary.

Bea: But is this all there is? I mean I feel a lot better, but this can't be the end of the counseling?

Doc: No, not at all. Actually, the counseling's off to a good start, but there's still quite a bit to do. Like I said in the first session, if you can learn what's really going on here and use it, the counseling will never end.

Bea: What do you mean by that?

Doc: I'll show you. . . . Each of you take a piece of this magic chalk, and I'll teach you what I strongly suggest you do for the rest of your lives. I gave them each an imaginary piece of chalk and then said: "Watch what I'm going to do. I'm drawing a circle in chalk on the floor around your two chairs. It's invisible to everyone but you. It's called a solving circle. Keep in mind that the circle is only a chalk line; you can step out anytime you wish. I also call it a marriage circle. In it are a husband and wife; that's obvious. But there's another entity that's also in the circle. Can you think of what that entity could be?"

Bea: What do you mean, entity?

Doc: I mean something in the circle. It's not a person, but it's very important. The truth is, it's more important than either of you. What do you think it is? (I pointed at the space between them.) There it is, right between you. What do you think it could be?

Another longer pause:

Jim: I don't know. I'm not good at guessing games.

Bea: Could it be our relationship?

Doc: Very close. . . . What exactly is your relationship?

Jim: Our marriage. . . . Is that what you're driving at?

Bea: Of course, it's our marriage. That's what you've been driving at all along. Are you saying that our marriage is more important than what I want? More important than what I want even when I'm right and he's wrong?

Jim: That's what you're saying, isn't it, Doc?

Doc: You're both correct. The marriage is more important than either of you. Anyone who wants to have a strong happy marriage has to subordinate what he or she wants to the marriage. You did it here last week when you answered question five. You've just done it for a week in San Francisco. Marital problems are difficult. You know that. You struggled for three years with what Jim did, and I think you were worse off when you came in than you were when the problem started. It's amazing to me the marriage held together at all. You may not realize it, but I think you love each other very much.

When I said this, Jim reached over and hugged Bea. And she took his hand and kissed it. This kind of thing often happens when the couple has had a good week for the first time in years, but Bea was still doubtful.

Bea: But it's too simple. It's got to be more complicated. I've been angry for three years. I feel good right now, but I don't think it's going to last.

Doc: It's the simplicity that makes it so powerful. It'll last as long as you get into the circle whenever you have a problem. But maybe this question will help. Last week, when I was asking you the questions, you seemed a little irritated with me when I tried to get you to stick to what I asked. I wonder, did you think I wasn't on your side? Like I didn't care as much as you thought I should?

Bea: Yeah, that was my feeling exactly. I came here for help and I thought, *He's asking stupid questions, and he's insensitive to my feelings.*

Jim: I wasn't as ticked off as Bea, but I did wonder if you knew what you were doing.

Doc: You came for help. But you really weren't ready to get help. What you wanted is what most people want when they enter marriage counseling. You wanted me to be the judge and decide who was at fault. Doesn't everyone ask friends and family to support their position? You expect them to be on your side. Now here's the critical question: Tell me, whose side did you think I was on?

Bea: You weren't on my side. I mean, I wanted to get some things straight when you asked the first question, and you shut me up. To tell you the truth, I'm not sure you're on my side now.

Jim: I agree with Bea; you sure didn't seem to want to listen to what she had to say. I wondered about that. Isn't it your job to listen to what we have to say?

Bea flashed Jim a look of approval when he supported her. Another good sign. I answered:

Doc: You're right, both of you. I'm really not on either of your sides. No matter what you say or do, I'll never take sides. But I am on a very important side. What side do you think I'm on?

There was a long pause while this question sank in. I just waited. Finally, Bea said:

Bea: I don't understand. Is this another trick question?

Doc: It's just the opposite of a trick question. If this counseling is going to work, it's the only side I can be on.

Bea: Are you trying to tell us it's our marriage? You're on the side of our marriage?

Jim: Makes sense to me.

Doc: That's right, I am. Remember the first question, Are you here because you really want help for your marriage? That coming here is not a prelude to divorce?

They both nodded. What I was talking about now seemed especially to interest them.

Doc: Before you answered that question, you did a lot of sniping at each other. You were trying to get me to take sides. I said to myself, *Here they are, an unhappy husband and wife, more ready to pick on each other than to try to get some help*. But I thought, *Where's their marriage?* You didn't have your marriage with you. My concern was and is for your marriage. I'm desperately trying to teach you to be more concerned about it, too.

Bea: It's that third entity—our marriage—isn't it? As long as each of us acted like what we wanted was more important than our marriage, we didn't have a chance.

Jim: I never thought this would work, but it makes sense.

Bea: But I gave in. He didn't give in at all. Does this mean that I'll always have to give in?

Doc: Okay, you did; you gave in when you answered questions four and five. But you didn't give in to him. What did you give in to?

Bea: I get it. I gave in to the marriage. I guess this's the whole point of what you're trying to do. Isn't it?

Doc: That's right. No matter how difficult things get, all either of you can do is offer to do whatever you believe will make your marriage better.

Bea: In the marriage circle, I just tell him what I can do to help solve the problem?

Doc: Yes, but you do a lot more as well. You try to prevent problems from happening in the first place. You make a real effort to stop doing the things that have dominated your marriage for at least the past three years. What didn't you do to each other last week in San Francisco when you had such a good time?

Jim: I didn't complain or criticize her. And I stopped blaming. She didn't nag or bring up the affair; it was like getting out of jail.

Bea: I said I wouldn't, and I didn't. But it wasn't easy. But if you'd treat me all the time like you did last week, everything would be fine.

Doc: No, not treat you, treat your marriage. Get rid of the seven deadly habits that, given enough time, will put an end to any relationship.

Jim: Seven habits?

Doc: Right, *criticizing, blaming, complaining, nagging, threatening, punishing,* and *bribing*. Get rid of those habits and get in the marriage circle instead. You can have the good marriage you told me you wanted when you answered question one. Keep in mind there're no exceptions to the rule: *You can only control your own behavior.*

What couples learn when they use the marriage circle or solving circle is a basic axiom of choice theory: Never say or do anything in a relationship that experience tells you will drive you further apart. Do or say only what will bring you closer or keep you close. If you pay attention, you immediately know the difference.

Bea: But why couldn't we figure this out ourselves?

Doc: That's an important question. But don't feel bad that you couldn't. Almost no one in the world we live in seems to be able to figure this out. Look at all your married friends. I'll bet not one of them has the slightest idea about what you've just learned.

Jim: Friends, hell; both our parents are still married, and all they do is fight. That's why they like the kids to come; it gives them an excuse to stop fighting.

Bea: You can say that again.

Doc: If you want the complete answer to why you couldn't figure out what to do on your own, read

> a book called *Choice Theory*. I personally guarantee it. Here's a copy. Read it slowly together and talk about what you're reading. If you have any questions, call me. I'll be happy to hear from you.

As explained in *Choice Theory*, almost every marriage or any other relationship that falls apart does so because one or both partners uses external control psychology on the other. Because this is the world's psychology, strong loving marriages are hard to find anywhere. If either one of the partners is dissatisfied, using external control is like throwing gasoline on a fire to put it out. And like most external-control solutions, divorce is usually not the answer most couples want.

The best solution to marital unhappiness is not always divorce. And it isn't the marriage counseling I used with Bea and Jim either. The best solution would be to offer a way for all married couples or people who are about to get married to learn choice theory. This is a real window of opportunity; it could save many a marriage that is now doomed to fail, no matter how well it started. As long as couples use external control, marital failure is as predictable as a Greek tragedy.

5

JEFF

Mrs. Green sucks, English sucks. If you say you're glad to see me, you suck, too. There isn't an adult in the whole world who's glad to see me.

Jeff represents a huge group of lonely children and adolescents who have been disconnected by the external control psychology they have been exposed to, often at home, almost always in school. I believe they can be reconnected in school if the staff is careful to avoid any use of external control in their contact with these students.

If Jeff can't achieve a satisfying relationship with a responsible adult, he has almost no hope for a happy life. Our jails, prisons, divorce courts, and child protection agencies are filled with Jeffs and their female equivalents. Because the primary burden of caring for children falls more heavily on women, women have evolved a stronger need to love and belong than have men. And generally, they have less of a need for power, so they are more able to connect, at least with each other, than men.

Jeff's frequent use of the word *sucks* to describe the world he lives in tells how disconnected he is. Although he has learned to read at grade level, he has the potential for school failure, violence, drug abuse, sexual misconduct, and even suicide. He hasn't an inkling of what a good relationship with a responsible adult may be. He has friends, but they are as disconnected as he is. His friends exist mostly to support the destructive and self-destructive choices they make when they hang out together. Jeff cannot even conceive of the caring and support of a responsible friend.

At fourteen, Jeff sees the whole world as a conspiracy to control him. Since he was young, he has been the victim of external control psychology; the only thing he can count on is criticism, punishment, and rejection. Because he hates school, he has been just barely making it since the fourth grade, when he did well. He loves violence in movies and on television. He's been smoking since he was nine and is very interested in addictive drugs. He was rejected by his father, who disappeared when he was three years old. And though his mother tries, she is severely disconnected herself. Jeff and his mother spend the time they are together screaming at and threatening each other.

There would be some hope for Jeff if he could get a job. But to succeed at any job, now or later, he will have to be lucky enough to work for a person who will tolerate his early misbehavior and deal with him kindly, rather than with threats. But at fourteen or any age, this possibility is very unlikely to occur. The only other people who might save him are school personnel, perhaps a counselor working with one or two of his teachers. Given the way Jeff behaves in school, this, too, is unlikely to happen. But it is his only real chance.

To help him, both his counselor and teachers have to avoid any talk of control: any criticizing, blaming, threatening, and punishing. Jeff is supersensitive to external control psychology. As soon as he detects that anyone at school is trying to control him, even with rewards, he turns against the person. The external control psychology of the world has done a good job on Jeff. All any administrator, counselor, or teacher can do that has any chance of helping him is to try to make a relationship through the total avoidance of external control of any kind. Until the counselor and later a few teachers make that connection, it will be almost impossible to talk to him about changing the way he chooses to live his life.

In this instance, I will assume the role of the school's assistant principal. Jeff has been sent to my office frequently, so I know him. By using choice theory, all I am going to do is try to connect.

I'll start by saying, "Jeff, Mrs. Green sent you to see me. I'm glad she did. I'd like to talk to you for a little while. I never seem to have enough time, but today I do."

You may have noticed that I avoided all talk of what he did in class that led him to be sent to see me. Or any threats of what is going to happen to him if he keeps doing what he is doing every day. If I can continue to do so, I have a chance of establishing the relationship we must have if I am to help him.

"Mrs. Green sucks, English sucks. If you say you're glad to see me, you suck, too. There isn't an adult in the whole world who's glad to see me."

"I'm an adult, and I'm glad to see you. I think it's my fault that we haven't really talked. I'd like to hear what's on your mind."

"If I start telling you what's on my mind, you'll call the cops. I hate this school; it's like a prison. If you really want to help me, get me out of here. The idea of spending two more years in this cage blows my mind."

"I agree with you completely. That's why I want to talk. Like we're talking now. It's good."

"Good for what? Why don't you just give me detention and get it over with. That's what's going to happen anyway."

"I'm not going to punish you. I don't really know what to do that'll help, but I know that punishment's not going to work. Tell me, what was going through your mind when you got up this morning."

"What kind of crap is that question? The only thing on my mind is how much I hate going to this school. It sucks, everything sucks."

What I'm trying to accomplish is a conversation with Jeff in which I do nothing to control him. He may never have had this experience with any adult in the schools he's attended.

"What else do you hate?"

"What do you mean? I hate a lot of things. Like I said, the whole world sucks. What's to like?"

"What's to like? That's a good question. Is there anything that you like right now?"

"Yeah, I like to party. And I like to play a little hoop. That's about it."

"Have you ever liked a schoolteacher?"

He thought a little while about that question. The fact that he thought at all is encouraging.

"Not for a long time. But one I did. My fourth-grade teacher. She was cool; she wasn't always on my back."

Not using any external control behaviors, such as criticizing, blaming, complaining, threatening, or punishing, has taken him to where he has a good word for a teacher. It didn't take that long and, in my experience, it usually doesn't. But however long it takes, we've got to get there. No shortcuts here.

"I'll bet you remember something you did in there."

"She was always making us write. But she read some of the stuff I wrote, and she liked it. All the papers came back with things like 'Very good! or 'How did you think of that?' She was always encouraging; she said keep working until you say what you want to say."

Now I'm where I want to be. He's talking about something positive that he did in school and a teacher who helped it to happen. We're at the very beginning of a connection. My keeping totally away from external control is starting to pay off. His attitude and language when he said, "I like to party" were all red flags. He waited for external control to zap him and didn't get it. I didn't even raise my eyebrows. I passed that little test. But he'll keep testing, that I can count on.

"Do you ever write in class now?"

"For her? Get real. She fills my papers with red marks. I don't think Shakespeare could please her."

Shakespeare, that's an interesting reference. Whenever a school-hating kid uses an educational reference, it's encouraging. What I've got to do is continue on this tack. Then I've got to handle why he came to see me. I'll assume we made a small connection, and I'm now ready to send him on to class. The bell's just about to ring, so he can go to his next class. But if I'm not careful with how I let him go, he may just see me as another controlling person.

"I guess its time for you to go to your next class. I've enjoyed talking with you. I'd like to do it again."

"Yeah, thanks, man. I was hoping I wouldn't have to go back to English. My next class is art; I like to draw. But how about Mrs. Green, what're you going to do about her kicking me out of class?

"Nothing, nothing at all. I'm not going to do anything because I don't know what to do. You handle it. If she asks you what I did, tell her we had a talk and that I sent you to your next class. It's the truth. And I've enjoyed talking with you Jeff; that's the truth, too.

I have worked in schools enough to know that what I just said will ruffle some feathers—that some people will think I'm letting Jeff get away with something. But I'm not. Jeff had a talk with me, and we made a connection. The more we connect, the better chance he has to start working in school. Just by Jeff's mention of Shakespeare, I know he has the brains to do well if he wants to. But as long as he keeps being punished, he'll stay disconnected and do less than he's doing now. He'll go from breaking school rules to breaking the law, and there's a good chance he'll end up in prison or dead at an early age. We need to deal with him successfully before he commits a crime. But that means some of us will have to stop using external control while we can still do it. Once he gets in the totally external control hands of the law, it'll be too late. This positive meeting with an authority figure and our beginning to connect is good, but Jeff also needs to connect with a teacher like Mrs. Green. I'm on good terms with her; I have to talk with her and feel her out about taking a choice-theory tack with Jeff.

"What if she kicks me out again? Two more times, and I flunk."

This question is interesting and hopeful; Jeff cares enough about school to mention that he doesn't want to flunk. As much as these kids seem to hate school and teachers, a lot of them would turn around if we could get rid of the external control. Jeff now thinks I'm worth telling this to. On the basis of what we've been talking about, there's a part of him that *wants* to pass.

"Well, we've started talking, I want to keep talking, to get to know you. You don't have to be kicked out of class to talk to me. If it's okay with you, I'll call you in when I get some free time. It may be every day even if sometimes it's only for a few minutes. If you think you can figure out how to stay in there for a few days, I'd like to talk to Mrs. Green. I'll tell her about your fourth grade teacher; maybe she'd like to encourage you a little, too."

This is a little external control, but I won't get to first base with Mrs. Green if Jeff can't control himself in her class for a few days. I've got to tell him that. I've done this enough that I think he'll give it a try. If he doesn't, well, I'll do the best I can with her.

Let's skip to a meeting a few days later with Mrs. Green. I told her to stop by this afternoon for a few minutes to talk to me about Jeff. She came in, but she was not very friendly. She started in immediately.

"I'm upset with you. I sent Jeff to you the other day, and you know what he told me? He said you didn't know what to do, so you didn't do anything. What kind of a thing is that to say to a kid like Jeff?"

"He told you that?"

"Do you think I'm making it up?"

"No, no. It's the truth; that's exactly what I told him. I'm just surprised he told it to you."

"If that's the truth, what's gotten into you? Have you lost it? What goes?"

"What goes is, it's the truth. I don't know what to do with Jeff, and I told him so. No one in this whole state knows what to do with Jeff. Do you?

"Well, I know one thing. Letting him get away with disrupting my class is the wrong thing to do."

"How's he been for the past two days?"

"Well, I haven't had to kick him out, if that's what you're asking. But I'll tell you, that kid's no good."

"If you're right that he's no good and you're right that I've lost it, what good does it do to send him to me? I think we can reach him. We've had a talk, a good talk. Have you ever tried to talk with him?"

"Look, I'm a teacher, not a counselor. I've got twenty-nine kids in there. I don't have time to talk to any of them. I give them something to do, and some of them do it. Some of them try pretty hard. Jeff doesn't do anything. I wouldn't mind it if he were quiet about it, but he's not. His mouth is going all the time. I'm sick of him."

"Would you ask him to write something? Anything, maybe three sentences, that's all."

"I ask them all to write. He hasn't written anything yet. Why should he start now?"

"Because he told me that when he was in the fourth grade, he used to write and the teacher encouraged him. I wonder if you'd try that. I mean figure out something he could write about and ask him to do it for you. It'd take you ten seconds, what've you got to lose? If he writes anything, write 'good' on it and send him to me with the paper. I want to see him as soon as he does."

"Okay, I get what you're doing. I hate to come across like I just did. I appreciate that you're trying to care about him. I know that's what he needs. Don't you think I know what's going on? Will you keep seeing him if I work with him? To tell you the truth, he's a smart kid. He could do something. It's so tough around here that sometimes I just want to give up."

Mrs. Green needed the attention I gave her just as much as Jeff did. She's a good teacher, a good human being, but she's over her head with kids as desperate for attention from adults as Jeff is. With choice theory, there's a lot that could be done for Jeff. With external control, he's finished. I worked with a middle school full of Jeffs for a whole school year, 1994–95, in Cincinnati and replaced external control with a lot of choice theory. The change worked some minor miracles. External control in school was killing those disconnected kids. The account appears in Chapter Ten of the book, *Choice Theory,* where I tried to show the difference between an external-control and a choice-theory approach. It wasn't reality therapy, but it was what had to be done before we could even think of using reality therapy.

6

CHELSEA

There's got to be something wrong with my brain. The way this happens, so sudden, no rhyme or reason, it can't be psychological.

This case both illustrates and explains my contention that we choose essentially all our behavior. But this explanation cannot be understood unless I expand the word *behavior* into two words: *total behavior*. Although I do not always use both words when I speak or write—it would be too cumbersome—whenever I think of behavior, I always think of both words. *In my mind, all behavior is total behavior.*

Suppose that as I was writing, you came in and asked me what I was doing. I would answer, "I'm writing," and you would be satisfied. But from a choice-theory perspective, that single word would not be correct. To be accurate, I would say, "I'm choosing to write." But that degree of accuracy is not usually necessary in ordinary conversation; the one word, *writing*, works fine. But suppose you came in right after I accidentally lost twenty pages of hard work from my computer. I'm sure you would find me feeling miserable and staring at the blank computer screen. You might ask, "What's wrong?" If we both knew choice theory, I would answer, "I'm depressing [or "I'm choosing to depress"] because I lost a day's work; I'm miserable."

The difference between the two examples is that writing describes an *activity,* whereas depressing describes a *feeling*.

Almost everyone accepts that writing is chosen. But almost no one believes that when a person like Chelsea says, "I suffer from panic attacks," she is choosing that complaint. While all reality therapists understand total behavior, Chelsea does not and would take exception if I told her she is choosing to panic. I would never tell her she was choosing to panic until I believed she was ready to understand total behavior. To do so would be harmful to the relationship I am trying to create with her.

But in counseling, I would use the concept of total behavior to help Chelsea make a better choice than to panic. And if she chose to stop panicking, I would begin to explain how she could use the concept of total behavior to choose more satisfying behaviors for the rest of her life. But in counseling, the concept of total behavior should be used with caution. No one should use it to accuse anyone of choosing the misery he or she is complaining about. Therapy depends for its success on clients making better choices—choices that help them and don't hurt anyone else.

Choice theory explains that all behavior is made up of four distinct but inseparable components: *acting, thinking, feeling,* and the *physiology* that accompanies the other three. For example, reading, which is the total behavior you're choosing now, is made up of *acting* (holding the book and turning the pages), *thinking* (absorbing the written material), *feeling* (what you feel as you read), and *physiology* (what your body is doing on its own as you read).

In this chapter, Chelsea is *choosing* the total behavior of *panicking,* but she has no idea what total behavior is or that it is a choice. When she first came in, she was nowhere near ready to understand this concept. But I believe that after we talk over her life and begin to work toward solving her frustrations, she will choose to stop panicking and I can begin to explain why she panicked and what she can do about it.

The reason most people find the idea that total behavior is chosen so difficult to understand is that all we can choose are two of the four components: our *actions* and *thoughts*. We can choose only these two components because they are the ones that are under our voluntary, conscious control. If we wish to change a total behavior, we must *change the way we act and/or think*. No matter what total behavior we choose, if we are willing to make the effort, we can choose to act and/or think in more satisfying ways. If I am successful in helping Chelsea, she will choose to act and think more effectively.

Why one frustrated person will panic, another will obsess, and still another will depress or choose another symptom is not yet known. What is known is that these disturbing choices reduce pain. Hard as this may be to believe, the frustration would be more painful if the person did not make this particular choice. As much as she complains about her panic attacks. Chelsea would suffer more if she didn't choose them.

When she came to see me, it was important for me to know that her fear and her racing heart are the appropriate feelings and physiology for the total behavior, panicking. But even though I know it's a choice, I'll certainly not dismiss her complaints, I'll give her time to explain how she feels. But I will also begin to work on guiding her *toward choosing different, more need-satisfying, actions and thoughts*.

I downplay her feelings and physiology because no therapy or therapist can work directly with feelings and physiology. For example, it would do no good to tell Chelsea to *get a grip* or to *cheer up*. As long as her needs are not satisfied, she won't be able to do so. When she begins to satisfy her needs through acting and thinking effectively, specifically to improve the relationship that's not working for her, the panic attacks will stop. (For a more detailed description of total behavior, see Chapter Four of *Choice Theory*.)

Chelsea is typical of clients who feel pain and discomfort in that she didn't mention the actions and thoughts she was choosing when she told me about the panic attacks. She concentrated solely on the feelings and the physiology: the terror, the cold sweats, her pounding and accelerating heart, and her loss of strength in her arms and legs. It is certainly true that her complaints are real, but she can't change them. None are under her direct, voluntary control.

You will see that as I counsel Chelsea, I pay a lot of attention to her as a capable person and as little as possible to the panic attacks she is complaining about. Recognizing her, despite the "attacks," is crucial to the success of the therapy. After she registers her complaints, I will pay less attention to them because I know that neither she nor I can do anything that will directly stop them. My focus will be on what she wants in her life that she could achieve by changing the way she acts and thinks.

Although some critics call this approach cold and unfeeling, I disagree. Our job as therapists is to teach clients how to act and think more effectively so they can better satisfy their needs, not to support their unrealistic hope that therapy or therapists can rid them of painful feelings or uncomfortable physiology.

You can talk to a client about her feelings and physiology forever, and nothing will change. Furthermore, the more you talk about these involuntary components, the more clients hope that the therapist or therapy can make them feel better, something no therapist or therapy can do. The only thing that can make anyone feel better, without acting and thinking more effectively, is to take addicting drugs or feel-good medications, such as Prozac. Neither is a permanent solution.

To illustrate, let me go back to the example of you reading this book. You can continue to sit and read, or you can close the book and leave the room. You can do almost anything you want as long as it can be accomplished by choosing different actions and thoughts. But what you can't do is put the book down and choose to panic or to feel ecstatic or any other emotion or physiology directly without concurrently changing your actions and thoughts. You can't, and Chelsea can't. If I am to help her or any other client, I have to focus on what she *can* change: her actions and thoughts.

Picture an attractive thirty-one-year-old woman, and you have Chelsea. She is well educated, has a job she loves, and has lived for four years with her boyfriend Tim. She and Tim plan to be married in six months. Chelsea's life seemed to be without serious problems until three months ago when she started to "experience" what have been diagnosed as panic attacks. These attacks have happened at various times, but so far not while she's driving. They have occurred with friends at lunch, while visiting her parents, and in the small friendly grocery store where she shops. They even occur at night while she is in bed with Tim. Chelsea lives in constant fear of an attack. So far she has not had one at work. Once or twice she's felt the quick panicky feeling she gets just before an attack. But that's all. It's never progressed into an attack.

Work, she says, is very satisfying. It's one of the real bright spots in her life. She has been given some psychiatric medication by her family doctor, but when the attacks continued, he advised her to see a counselor. Her employee assistance plan at work will pay for ten visits, so she's come to see me. During the first visit, she told me all that I've written here. With that in mind, let's now start her second session.

"What's wrong with me? How could my doctor ask me to see a counselor? There's got to be something wrong with my brain. The way this happens, so suddenly, no rhyme or reason, it can't be psychological. People with psychological problems are miserable; they don't have all the good things I have going for me. I'm at my wits' end, what can you possibly do for me?"

Here you can see how unaware she is that her attacks are the feeling and physiology components of the total behavior, panicking. At this point, I have to be careful not even to imply that she's choosing these attacks.

"I'll talk with you. I'm sure I can help you for the very reason you just said: You have so much going for you. There can't be that much wrong in your life."

"But if there's nothing wrong, why the attacks?"

"I didn't say there was nothing wrong. There is something wrong. But you have so much going for you that it may not be hard to correct."

I paused after I said that and looked at her. She just said her life was fine. I've just said something's wrong, and now she looks as if an attack is coming on. I immediately dealt with that observation.

"Do you feel as if you are going to have an attack right now?"

"How did you know? I do feel a little fearful, the way I do before an attack."

"Please don't try to stop it for me. I'd like to see you while you're having an attack. You told me they go away after a while, but I'd like to have a chance to talk with you while it's going on."

"But it's awful; I can hardly talk."

"You won't have to say much. I'll ask questions, and you'll just nod yes or no."

I say this matter-of-factly, as if it's no big deal. If she thinks I can handle the attack, she won't choose to have one in my office. If I'm not afraid of it and even welcome it, she can't control me with it as I'm sure she controls others. So it's unlikely she'll choose to have one now. It's more likely that the attack will occur just before or after she sees me. Because I do not fear her threatened attack, she knows I don't think the attacks are as mysterious or difficult to deal with as she thinks they are. If she is choosing them to impress people, I'm not impressed.

"But aren't you supposed to prevent these attacks? Why are you talking so casually about my having one? They're horrible. I don't want to have another one if I can help it."

Indirectly, she is talking about gaining control over the attacks, and that's good. Now I have to get to the unsatisfying relationship. I'll probe into what she means when she says things in her life are fine except for the attacks. First, I'm going to try to find out how she and Tim are getting along, since some aspect of that relationship is most likely the source of these attacks.

"You've been living with Tim for quite a while without setting a date to get married. Now you've finally set one. Who's been hesitating, you or Tim?"

"Neither of us; we just want to make sure. He loves me. We've been living together for almost four years. It's about time, isn't it?"

"And you love him?"

"Of course, I do. Why else would I be getting married?"

"Marriage is a lot more than loving each other. It's making a big commitment, changing the way you live your life, maybe having children and a new home and money problems. It's not at all like living together. . . . When did the attacks start?"

This is not going back into the past. The attacks are part of the present. I may be able to use the information about how long they've been going on.

"I told you, about three months ago."

I ask this question again because I'm trying to find out if there is a relationship between setting the wedding date and the attacks.

"When did you set the date to get married?"

"I don't know exactly, quite a while, about six months ago. That's it, I remember. It was six months ago when he gave me this ring."

"Tim is serious. No question about it; that's an exceptional diamond."

"Tim likes to do everything in a big way. He's so alive; I love that about him. But if you think that getting married is the problem, why didn't the attacks start sooner?"

"I'm not blaming the attacks on the fact that you're planning to get married. I don't know what the problem is. I'm just asking questions."

"I want to get married, and so does Tim."

There it is. By what she read into my questions, I think I'm on the right track. She went on to reassure me, but I also believe she was reassuring herself. I'll go back to the question that she avoided and ask it in a slightly different way.

"This may seem like a funny question, but I wonder if you could try to answer it. Who wants to get married the most, you or Tim?"

"We set the date together."

"I'm sure you did. But it's not uncommon when people have been living together as long as you have that one wants it more than the other."

"Oh, I see what you mean. He does; he's been after me for the past year that it's time we got married. He's older than me, forty-three, and he wants to buy a house and start a family. He's a stockbroker; he makes a lot of money. He wants me to stop working. Become a lady of leisure. My mother and father are crazy about him. They're delighted with the idea that we're finally going to settle down."

"Sounds like a done deal. You don't have any concern that this might be a mistake?"

"I've got some qualms; every woman has qualms in a situation like this."

"Tell me one qualm."

"I like my job. I'm a librarian. It doesn't pay much, but I enjoy every minute I'm there. The job of head children's librarian is open, and I've interviewed for it. Tim just doesn't understand how I can enjoy sitting in a library for the rest of my life, but I really love it. It's the only thing we don't agree on. But, my God, are you saying that these attacks could come from something as simple as that?"

"I told you, I don't know. But your job in the library is not simple. It's the most important thing you do outside of living with Tim, and he doesn't understand why it's so important. When you think of leaving this job, what goes through your mind?"

"What's going through my mind is I don't want anymore of these attacks. They're terrible. I've gotten to the point where all I think about is having them. I've stopped thinking about anything else."

I had to persist here. She evaded that question about leaving her job. That job is very important to her, and Tim doesn't understand its importance.

Very gently I said, "But please, when you think about leaving the library, how do you feel? It seems to be a safe place; you don't have any attacks there."

"I don't want to leave the library. I feel sad."

"Sad and panicky?"

"No, just sad. If I get married, I may have to leave."

"Let me teach you something. When you have a frustration in your life and there seems to be no way to deal with it, you can try to put it out of your mind. And sometimes you can. But not always. Instead of getting it out of your mind, it goes underground. Your brain keeps working on it without you even knowing. And one of the ways your brain works on frustration is to change the way you feel and even the way your body functions. These attacks may be one of the ways your brain is trying to help you keep your mind off giving up your library job. One of the two places you don't have an attack is at work, the place you most want to be and the place most threatened by getting married. And you're not suicidal; you don't have them while you're driving."

I'm sewing the seeds of total behavior, that she has some control over the attacks, since they don't occur at work or while she's driving.

"But once I felt one coming on and I pulled into a parking lot. It wasn't much of an attack, but I was really scared."

"That's what I just said; you don't have them when you're driving; you had the good sense to pull over. It seems to me that you may have a little control over them. My guess is you have them most when people are around—where people can see there's something wrong."

A major purpose of all psychological symptoms is to get sympathy and attention. That's why I guessed that Chelsea gets these attacks when she's with people.

"There's something to that. I've had five or six of them while I was talking on the phone with my mother."

"What were you talking about?"

"She was going on and on about my life after I get married. A big house, a family, lots of money, not having to work anymore."

I ventured a little further.

"Not much support there for staying on at the library."

"But I love him. I want to get married."

"If you love him, could you be honest with him? Bring up your feelings about the library. If he loves you, he'll make an attempt to understand."

Now I am able to focus on what she needs to become aware of—that she has to change some of her thoughts and some of her behavior.

"But I've tried. He just says it's impossible. He doesn't want 'his wife' to work."

"Do you want to get married and then defy him?"

"No, I've made up my mind that after we get married, I'll go along with quitting work. We'll have plenty of money."

"But you're here because of what's going through your mind before you're married. There's a big part of you that doesn't want to leave the library right now, maybe never. This is not a guess. You've made that very clear. You said your life is good. As you sit here now, calm and comfortable, why is it so good?"

"Well, I have what I want."

"Right. You have Tim and you still have your job in the library. Marriage could mess up your job. You don't want to face that, do you?"

"No, I really don't."

"Are you prepared to get married while you're still having these attacks?"

"Tim says the attacks will stop if we get married. He wants to marry me even with these attacks."

"What does Chelsea say?"

"I don't know. All I know is that right now I don't want to give up my job in the library. I really don't. The job hasn't hurt our relationship so far, how could it hurt it after we get married? Besides, if it did, I could always quit."

"Chelsea, you don't have a very big problem; you'll solve it. You're not going to have these attacks forever. I can help you."

"How'll you help me?"

"Go home and think about what we've talked about. Try to come to grips with what's so different about marriage from what you have now? Talk to Tim about it; see what he has to say."

Chelsea (third session):

"How'd the week go?"

"Not too bad. Just one little attack while I was talking to my mother. Really, a pretty good week."

"Did you talk to Tim?

"I talked to him. But it was as if he expected what I wanted. He was adamant. When we get married, he doesn't want me to work. His mind was so closed, I didn't argue; I don't like to argue. As soon as he got his way, he was so loving that I said to myself, *I love him, his way isn't that bad*. I felt good. But on the way over here, I had the feeling an attack was coming on. As soon as I got into the garage, it seemed to subside."

"Were you upset about telling me you had to give in to Tim?"

"I was. I was like a schoolgirl who hadn't done her homework."

"No, you did it. You tried."

"Maybe I tried. But I don't think I tried very hard. The thing is when I'm with him, the library doesn't seem so important. But when we're married and I'm home all day, I know I'm going to miss it. My God, all I want is one thing. I'm ready to leave the rest to him. I keep thinking. Am I really ready to give in on this? And how about the rest of our marriage? Am I giving up too much for love? You were right when you said that marriage is a lot different from living together. . . . It's my life, that's what the library represents. We're not even married, and he wants the one thing I don't want to give him. What's going to happen if we get married?"

"This is the time to try to answer that question."

"You see, Doctor, Tim's in love with money. Not like Ebenezer Scrooge, not that way at all. He's generous; I'd have all the money I'd ever want with him, but I get the feeling it'd be his money, not our money or my money. I like having my own money; it's not much, but it gives me a sense of independence I don't want to lose. Do you know what I'm saying? I keep trying to tell myself that it's all going to be fine. But right now I'm wondering if this is the marriage I really want."

"Are you willing to talk with him about this? I mean, to stand up for yourself and make this point no matter how loving he is or promises to be?"

"It'll be hard. He keeps telling me how much he loves me. That he wants to make money so he can share it with me. He's been talking to my mother; she's on his side one hundred percent. That's when I had that little attack. The idea that I might give up a rich, loving, good-looking guy for a job in the library is beyond her. But she's not the problem; I can deal with my mother. It's getting a lot clearer now."

I think it's time to ask a generic question about marriage. Tim sounds like Torvald, the leading character in Ibsen's play, *A Doll's House,* whose love for his wife was based on control. That marriage was a disaster.

"Chelsea, why are there so many unhappily married couples? You probably know a lot of them, some of them not even married very long."

"I don't know. After a while, they just don't get along. My folks got along when I was little. Then they fought for twenty years until they got tired of that. Now they get along okay—not great but okay. But I'll tell you, they're both dying for me to marry Tim."

"Right now, do you ever tell Tim what to do? I mean, where to go, what to wear, what to order in a restaurant. You're a librarian, do you tell him you'd like him to read a book so you can talk about it?"

"Tim gives the orders, not me. He even plans the menus."

"Has it increased in the time you've been together. I mean, his running the show."

"I don't know if it has. It's just been that way from the start. But it's so easy to let him run things. I mean, I have my job in the library. I come home tired, and he has things all under control; you know, brokers don't always work long hours. Dinner is started; he loves to cook. The wine's cooled to the right temperature. Life with Tim is good."

That's enough on her and Tim. There's nothing more to say.

"Okay, I think we've covered all the ground. What do you think you're going to do?"

"I guess I've really got to talk to him before we go any further. That's it, isn't it?"

I didn't answer that last question; this had to be her decision, not mine.

"What are you going to talk about."

"I'm going to tell him that I love him and that I'd like to marry him, but I'm not going to give up my job in the library. Not for the foreseeable future."

"He may drop you."

"No, I'm not worried about that. He won't drop me. . . . This may sound cold, but it isn't; it's a fact. Doctor, do you know what I am to Tim? I'm an investment. He has four years invested in me, and he takes good care of his investments. If you could see all he does to make me comfortable, you'd know how well he treats me. You know what I think, I think he'll agree. It'll come to him that letting me work is a good way to protect his investment—that a happy wife is a good wife.

"Sounds good to me."

"I'll explain how much I appreciate all he does for me now. Tell him what a great cook he is and how lousy a cook I am. I'll get through to him. The truth is, I've just never really stood up to him before. He'll be able to tell the difference in a moment. It's what I have to do, isn't it?"

I nodded in agreement. She'd made up her mind.

"I can deal with this. I appreciate your help. Can I call you if I need you?"

"I hate to keep saying this, but are you prepared to give him up if he won't agree?"

"He's no fool. He loves me. He'll think more of me for taking a stand. But the answer to your question is, yes. I'm prepared to lose him; he'll hear that in my voice. The thing is, if I lose him, I think I'm also going to lose my mother. Will you see her if she cracks up? I feel good. I doubt if I'm going to have any more attacks."

And that was it. Chelsea didn't have any more attacks. She and Tim got married. Chelsea was a strong woman. I think she knew she was strong; that's why she put up with all his control. If he wants to give her all that attention, why not take it? There are worse things than being controlled with a lot of attention. Everyone who comes for therapy is not a basket case. Chelsea just needed a little nudge to assert herself before she got married. I hear from her at Christmas. She now has two children, and she's been head children's librarian since before she got married. Life is not literature; it's okay to have a happy ending.

7

GEORGE

There was nothing about him that gave me even a hint of what he was going to say.

When I counsel George, you will see how knowledge of an important component of choice theory, the *quality world*, played a crucial role in what I decided to do. This small, simulated world that we begin to create in our memory shortly after birth and continue to create and adjust from birth until death is the core of our lives. In it, we store detailed memory pictures of people, things, and systems of belief that have satisfied our basic needs better than anything else.

For example, it would be hard to find more than a few people who didn't have a picture of their mothers in their quality world. We see ourselves loving our mothers and them loving us. Most of us can count on our mothers to help us satisfy our need for love. We all have pictures of other loved ones, some prized possessions, and some personal systems of belief that guide us as we make choices.

Our quality world is our personal Shangri-La, the place where we would want to live if we could access it in the real world. Every important thing we do from birth to death is always our best attempt to satisfy one or more pictures that we have either put into our quality world or are considering putting in. I need to explain this world before I start counseling George because if you don't understand it, what I do with George could be puzzling.

As stated earlier, each of us is driven by five genetic needs: *survival, love and belonging, power, freedom,* and *fun*. All our behavior, effective and ineffective, is always our best attempt at the time to satisfy one or more of these needs. For example, Melvin Udall could not figure out how to satisfy his need for love and belonging at the beginning of the film *As Good As It Gets*. Because he was frustrated, he was angering, the most common total behavior we choose when we are as disconnected as Melvin.

Melvin's choice to obsess and compulse, especially to avoid stepping on cracks, took so much effort that it protected him from lashing out as much as he would have if he hadn't had so many cracks to avoid. Almost all the symptoms we choose help us to restrain the anger that is a part of every frustration. If we couldn't restrain it, we could do harm to ourselves or others. In Melvin's case, blinded by his anger, he treated everyone badly and even threw the little dog, Fridell, down the rubbish chute.

Our quality world is the core of our lives because it is our direct motivation—where we always look when we are frustrated. If there is no picture to satisfy a need, we must try to create one; we cannot satisfy our needs directly. For example, no matter how lonely we are, we can't just go out and love. We need to find a specific person to love, as Melvin found Karen and Jerry found Carol. Although Jerry probably had a generic picture of a loving woman in his quality world for years, he couldn't fall in love until he could replace it with a specific picture: Carol.

Some of the work I do as a reality therapist is to teach clients how to find people who might help them satisfy their needs, especially the two most difficult to satisfy: love and power. We are all looking for people who love us and listen to us, people who soon become a part of our quality worlds. The same goes for things and systems of belief. But because finding satisfying relationships is our most common problem, that's where I concentrate my counseling. I bring the quality world up now because this chapter clearly illustrates how all-powerful a picture this world can be.

What we do, starting at birth and continuing all our lives, is pay special attention to any person, thing, or idea—often to a whole situation, such as a business or profession—that feels especially good. Or that we believe would feel especially good if we could connect with it. As much as many people try to deny the importance of feelings, they are, without doubt, our strongest motivator. In search of climber's ecstasy, many climbers attempt Mount Everest, a mountain that most dedicated mountain climbers put into their quality worlds as soon as they begin serious climbing.

But it is important to understand that the people, things, or ideas that we put into our quality world are not necessarily good or moral as the world generally defines these qualities. Alcoholics put alcohol into their quality worlds and keep it there even if it costs them their lives or their freedom. If Carol rejects Jerry, he may do her harm or even kill her because he doesn't want to take her out of his quality world. When their quality worlds are frustrated, rejected lovers can be dangerous. Attend a few operas if you don't believe me.

But in many instances, the most important picture in our quality worlds is the way we picture ourselves. All our lives we attempt to create pictures of ourselves satisfying our needs. For example, when he came to see me, Jerry did not have a clear, effective picture in his quality world of how to become intimate with Carol. Jeff, on the other hand, still had a picture of himself succeeding in school in his quality world, but he had no picture of anyone whom he trusted enough to help him do it.

It is important to know that we always control what we put into our own quality world. No one can force his or her way into it or escape from it without our permission. When a woman divorces her abusive husband, she usually wants him to take her out of his quality world. But sometimes he doesn't, and his failure to do so often leads to violence and even murder. All our lives we adjust and readjust our quality worlds on the basis of finding someone or something that feels better than before. We may labor for a lifetime to satisfy an important picture in our quality worlds.

But we also must understand that it is easier to put a picture into our quality worlds than to take a picture out. If we are rejected by someone we love, we can't usually get rid of that picture unless we find someone to replace it. If Carol rejects Jerry because of the way he chooses to behave (which she can't control), he may remain in her quality world for years if she can't find anyone better to replace him.

What clients are taught in therapy is to try not to make their own picture or the pictures of others in their quality worlds too difficult to satisfy. If you are tolerant of yourself and others, you will have a much better chance for happiness. Sometimes it is impossible to be tolerant, but it usually can be done.

Finally, there are millions of people who have no one in their quality worlds and are totally disconnected. Jeff could be such a person. Unlike an autistic person, as played by Dustin Hoffman in the movie *Rainman*, or Ted Bundy, the serial killer in real life, Jeff still wants to connect. But if he doesn't succeed in connecting, he may eventually take all people out of his quality world. When he does, he will become dangerous in that he will almost surely opt for violence to satisfy his need for power. Usually violence against others but sometimes against himself as in suicide. He may also choose drugs (he is already smoking marijuana) and engage in what I call nonloving sex—taking his pleasure no matter what his partner or victim wants.

With this in mind, I will now turn to George. George is forty-nine, pleasant looking, a little over average height, and slender. There is nothing distinctive about his appearance or how he dresses. When he called for an appointment, his tone of voice suggested pain and urgency, but that tone is so common with clients that I didn't think his problem was out of the ordinary. George didn't volunteer anything over the phone, and that was fine with me. I rarely ask clients what the problem is when they call for an appointment. He insisted that I see him as soon as possible.

I started the session by saying, "George, I've got plenty of time. When I get a call like yours I fit you in at the end of the day. Your voice and the way you talked led me to believe you're in a lot of pain. Maybe you're not the kind of person who turns to others for help. Coming here wasn't easy for you, was it?"

He agreed and I continued, "We can talk as long as you want. I called my wife and told her to go ahead with dinner. I'll eat later; no problem."

Then I looked at George as if I wanted to hear the story. There was a pause of about ten seconds, and then he started to talk.

"I've been thinking about coming for almost a year. But to look at my life, you'd think I'm the last person who would need to see a therapist. I'm the owner of a profitable travel agency that employs twenty-four people. I've been married to a good woman for twenty-seven years, and our one child, a young man of twenty-five, is already very successful on his own."

He then paused again and waited until he was sure he had my complete attention, "But I'll tell you, doctor, it's come to the point where I'm seriously thinking of killing myself. I live inside a black cloud only I can see. I get along well with all the people who are close to me—my wife, my son, and all my friends. I treat my employees very well and, literally, everyone likes me. And I like them. I'm not a loner or anything like that. My wife has no inkling of what I'm going through. If she had any idea I was considering suicide, she would totally decompensate. She thinks everything is fine. I can't begin to tell her what's going on inside my head. I can't tell anyone. Last week, I bought a gun. It was when I did that, that I said to myself, *I won't wait any longer; I'll go see a psychiatrist.* A while ago, someone mentioned you in a conversation, and I thought, *Maybe him?* I don't know anyone else, and the way you were mentioned was favorable."

After he told me that story, he paused. I think he wanted me to say something, but I didn't know what so I kept quiet. But two words he used interested me: "decompensate" and "favorable." My guess is he's a thoughtful person who keeps his feelings to himself. But there was also a forbidding air about him as if he was the kind of person who could try, convict, and then execute himself. An emotional person would not have chosen to speak to me in that flat intellectual way and would have used less precise language.

I didn't say anything, so he continued, "When I made the appointment, I said to myself, *If he can't help me, it's all over.* My affairs are in good shape and, besides, I have a substantial insurance policy. I took it out two years ago when these suicidal thoughts began to increase; they've been there for a long time. The policy will pay off for suicide; it's past the time when the actuaries believe a person can plan to do it."

Again the meticulous planning and the use of the words *substantial* and *actuaries.* Grasping at anything I could think of, I said, "How much time has to pass before they will pay off for suicide?"

"Six months; I'm safe."

Something is very unusual here. He has all the surface reasons to be happy, but he's miserable. I just have to keep quiet and listen; he's going to explain this mystery. If my theory is correct, regardless of his seeming closeness to his family and friends, his need for love and belonging is severely frustrated. His actions with people are a front; he feels little or nothing for most of them. Ideas of suicide often occur when people can't connect with a very important picture in their quality worlds. He is depressing very strongly; that black cloud represents his choice to depress. There has to be something in his quality world that he has absolutely no way to satisfy. What further comes to mind is that he may be indulging in the most disconnecting behavior anyone can choose: criticizing himself. When others criticize us, it may be difficult, but we can usually separate physically or mentally from them. When we criticize ourselves for being inadequate to deal with something pictured in our quality worlds, we may then consider taking ourselves out of our own quality worlds. If we do so, we have no more reason to live. That choice signals that our life is over. There is no time to waste. He is very close to ending it all.

"George, you came for help and, difficult as it is for you to believe in the frame of mind you're in, I think I can help you. But I can only help you if you're alive and if you'll tell me honestly what's on your mind. To begin, the way I see it, no matter what your problem is, I feel as if you're giving me the ultimatum: *Doctor, if you can't help me, I'm going to kill myself.* You seem so impatient, as if I've got to do something quick, or it's all over. It's almost as if you'd say to yourself, *I gave psychotherapy a try and it didn't work.* . . . George, are you using me? Is this visit going to allow you to leave a note saying you saw me and I couldn't help you?"

There was a long pause as he thought over what I said. I didn't say anything; I just looked at him. Finally, he said, "It's a little like that but not exactly. I've almost made up my mind that you can't help me. Rather than go through a long counseling process and end up no better off than I am, the best thing to do is to kill myself. But the door's not completely closed; it's still open a crack. But I'll tell you, I'm not here to include you in a note. I doubt very much if I'll even leave a note."

"Okay. The door's not closed. That's good. Could I persuade you to keep it open for a while longer? I have to be honest. I haven't the strength to start seeing you if I have to worry that at any moment you may end your life. My brain doesn't work well under that kind of pressure. If I'm to see you past today, I want something from you."

"What?

"I want you to give me as much time as you were willing to give the insurance company: six months. You seem to be a very business-like person. Sign a contract agreeing to come here once or twice a week for six months. I can't predict where we will be in six months, but I need that much time to start."

There was a long pause while he thought that over. Then he said, "You don't even know what's wrong. When I tell you, you may not want six months. You may not want to see me at all. How can you even think you can help me in six months or six years if you don't know what's wrong?"

"But that's just it," I said. "That's why I don't want to know right now. All I want is the six months. And I'll sign the contract, too. I don't want you to think that I'm going into this with any conditions or any reservations about my ability to deal with the problem. You've told me you're thinking of suicide. That's a psychological problem, no matter what the cause. There's nothing you can come up with that's going to cause me to renege on seeing you. And I have complete confidence if I see you, I can help you."

I say this because this is how I've felt with every voluntary client I've ever seen. He's not like Jeff. Teens like Jeff, and even adults who are forced into therapy, for example, as probationers, may be impossible to help. But George is different. Unless he's got something seriously wrong with his brain—a tumor or some rare genetic disease, such as Huntington's chorea—I should be able to help him. I share this confidence with all the clients I have seen, and I've never regretted it. People who come for therapy want to work with a counselor who has faith in the process and his or her ability to use it. If given enough time, I can help anyone who comes and asks for help. I worked successfully, on and off, for close to forty years with one potentially homicidal client who was seriously thinking of murder for much of the time I saw him. George seemed reassured.

"I'll sign the contract. It's a fair offer. I'm just warning you that I'm totally miserable. My life is all an act. I can't go on much longer."

"Good. You're a businessman. You write out the contract, and I'll sign it. But I want one more thing."

"What?

"Where's the gun right now?"

"It's in the trunk of my car. Why?"

"Because I want to go down to your car with you and bring it up here. I want to lock it in this desk drawer for as long as we see each other. Contract or not, I can't counsel effectively if that gun is in your possession."

"I could just get another one."

"If you start getting some help from me, you won't do that. No one can watch you day and night; in a moment of pain, you might use the gun. Once you pull that trigger, there's no turning back. In the old days, I would've even considered committing you to a psychiatric hospital, but you're far too sane. No judge would commit you no matter what I said. . . . But do you see the sense of giving me the gun?"

I thought what I just asked him to do would make sense to him, and it did. I can't counsel him if every time we meet I have to worry about saying something that he misperceives and uses as an excuse to break the contract. He thought so, too, and didn't put up any resistance. I did the same thing with the homicidal patient's guns, and it'd worked fine; I kept those guns locked in my office for years. We went down to George's car; I got the gun and locked it in my desk. George asked to use my word processor, and I gave him time to compose the contract right there. When he finished, we both signed it. But we still had plenty of time left, so I started in.

"Now, please tell me what's wrong. You can tell me things that you've almost been afraid to tell yourself. There's no hurry; we can take as long as you want."

He did take his time; minutes went by, and in my small office, they seemed to be an eternity.

Finally he said, "I want to be a woman."

There was nothing about him that gave me even a hint of what he was going to say. As much as I could, I tried to be cool and not act surprised. But I was. And as I thought about it, it all fit in. As much as he was living a normal life, he had a picture of himself in his quality world as a woman. For totally unknown reasons, once people put an opposite-sex picture into their quality worlds, they can't change it no matter how hard they may try. As we talked, George confirmed that the picture had been there since he was a young child. He had done his best to deny it. He had married, fathered a child, and built a successful business, but it could not be changed. Living what, to him, was a lie was tearing him apart. But after he told me, I could feel him relax just a little. He had me pictured in his quality world as someone he could tell this to who would not reject him, and he could see I was that person.

"Have you ever told anyone what you've just told me?"

"A few people. No one who really knows me, never my family or friends. You see, for a while I thought I was homosexual, so I had three of those contacts but they weren't satisfying at all. I hated what we did. I had to face the fact that I didn't want a man unless I was a woman. I did confide in them when they wondered why I didn't like what we were doing. One of them said, 'You ought to see a psychiatrist; you're all fucked up.' I've stopped that behavior, and I feel a little better about that. Besides, it's not just sex. I want to be a woman and do all the things that women do. If it was possible, I'd like to give birth to a child. I enjoy shopping for women's clothes; I rent a small office near work where I keep them—lot's of them. I go to that office for relief, but it's hardly satisfying. I want to look in a mirror and see a woman. I want to touch myself and not feel a penis. I'm a woman trapped in a man's body. But I'm not a freak. I'm a mistake. I know that people like me can get an operation, but it's more complicated than that. I'm not alone in the world. I've got a wife and son who love me. I've got parents who love me. I can't just disappear and resurface as a woman and say, 'Surprise!' How do I tell this to my wife, my son, my parents? If I had the operation, could I continue to run my business? Would my customers accept it? Would my employees? Would my banker accept it? It's not like I could talk to anyone and ask, *Would you accept me as Georgia instead of George?* And then if I had the operation, it might not work. All that's a good argument for suicide. You wouldn't deny that, would you?

I didn't take long to answer him. I didn't want to seem overwhelmed, I wanted to act as if I knew what to do because I was pretty sure I did.

"Your wife, son, and parents are the best argument for not killing yourself. Why do you think that everyone will automatically reject you if they knew about this? People can accept a lot if they know how a person they love is suffering."

"Okay, you may be right. But telling them, just thinking about it, turns me ice cold."

"George, cold or hot, a lot of what's going to happen now depends on you. I have to talk frankly; this is not the time to beat around the bush. If you decide to have the operation, the only thing that's going to change is your body. Your mind's been that way for years. While nothing's certain, your new body would finally be congruent with your mind."

"You're assuming I want the operation."

Since he can't change the picture of himself as a woman in his quality world, if he wants to relieve his suffering, he sees that his only choices are suicide or the operation. In my opinion, he's better off alive than dead, so the operation should be strongly considered.

"Of course I am. You've read up on your problem. You know all about the operation. What else could you want? If it was just you, you would have had it years ago when it first became available. I wonder what stopped you?"

My being matter-of-fact was reassuring to him. He wasn't here to be coy or play games. Try as he may, he can't reject the reality of his life. I'm a reality therapist, this is reality and he needs help.

"Two things, fear of the operation; it's irreversible. But much more, my wife, my child, my parents, my business. If I become a woman, it'll all change. How can I deal with all that's going to happen? I may lose every person I have in the world. And with no certainty at all that I'll find what I really want—a man to love me. You see what I'm up against?"

"George, I can't help you to stop wanting to become a woman. No one can do that. But I can help you with all the people you mentioned. That's what we have to talk about. This is a tough thing to do. I don't think you can do it by yourself."

"I know I can't. That's why I'm here."

"Tell me who in your life is the most important person, the person who would be most hurt by this information?"

This was a tough question. Instead of answering it directly, George changed the subject. This is a good sign. He knows who this crucial person is, but before he tells me, he wants to impress on me the fact that he cares a lot about this person, I hope not more than life itself.

"Doctor, I almost killed myself before I called you. I even did a couple of the Russian roulette routines. I spun the cylinder twice with one bullet in it and pulled the trigger with the gun in my mouth. When the gun didn't go off, I took it as some kind of an omen and called you. But believe me, when I think of telling her, it's still an attractive idea."

"Her is your wife?

"She's a lovely woman. She puts up with all my moods and tries to support me. Like I said before, she'd decompensate if she had any inkling of what I've told you. I'm worried about what she might do."

"Have you ever come close to telling her?"

"I wouldn't say close, but I've thought about it."

"Before or after the operation? There could be an argument for either way."

"I'd want to tell her before. I'd want her there with me. I love her desperately, but not as a wife. I kind of see myself after the operation as a long-lost cousin who comes into her life just after I disappear forever."

He really has done some thinking about this. He's asking a lot of his wife, but if she loves him she may do it. It's not impossible.

"If I knew that she'd stop loving me after the operation, I couldn't bear it. I really do want the operation, but that's what I'm worried about."

"You're asking a lot of her."

"I know I am. That's where you come in. I need your help. Would you help me tell her? I don't think I could do it on my own. I'd break down and mess everything up."

"You can count on me to help, but I can't predict how she'll deal with it. We'll have to talk a lot more but not now; there're other things you have to do before we even think of telling her. How about your son?"

"I'm not so worried about him. If my wife accepts me, I think he will, too. I'd want to tell him, but maybe doing that could wait until it's over. Or maybe his mother will tell him. I just don't believe he'll reject me. I have no guilt where he's concerned. I've been a good father; I've never had any problem with that. We've been close. . . . It'll shake him, but he'll deal with it. He isn't married, so he won't have to cope with a wife or in-laws."

"How about your parents?"

"I have no idea, but I'm not worried about them. It's my wife; she's the one I'm worried about."

He has good reason to worry. This is about as hard a decision as a woman has to make. I've never been involved in anything like this. But I can make some calls around. I can find a psychiatrist who has some experience with this issue. The more I know, the better I'll be able to help him. I could turn him over to someone else, but we've made a good connection. He may think I am afraid to deal with his problem, and we'll lose the connection. It's that connection that's all important. Even his wife will look for that connection—that I really want to help him; that I respect him even though he wants to be a woman. This'll help her to deal with it. And I do feel connected. I feel the pain he's going through. Besides, I'm fascinated. George is a very interesting client.

"Let me ask you a tough question. Suppose I help you talk to your wife and she won't accept what you want to do. To use your words, suppose she decompensates, maybe attempts suicide, will you still go ahead with the operation?"

"I don't know what I'd do. I can't predict my behavior. I may go ahead and kill myself. You're the psychiatrist, what do you think she'll do?"

"I may be a psychiatrist, but I can't predict what anyone will do. I probably shouldn't have asked you that question."

This is a ticklish situation. I shouldn't have asked him that question, and he had every right to turn it back to me. But therapy is not perfect. Psychiatrists make mistakes like everyone else. I handled that mistake by admitting it and learning something from it. When I admit a mistake, it makes me more human and increases the connection. If I don't admit it, I risk harming our connection or looking stupid. My experience is that people can face almost anything if they are prepared for it and have the ability to love, as George's wife seems to love him. Then I thought of something I wanted to check out. As I do therapy, these thoughts come to me all the time. I wanted to give him some more support and to tell him indirectly that I support his idea of actually making the change. That killing himself may not be sensible, no matter what his wife decides to do. I also wanted to get off the subject of his wife. I didn't think conjecturing any more about her was the thing to keep doing.

After a pause that would prepare him for changing the subject, I said, "If you killed yourself now, before you told anyone, who would you be killing, George or Georgia?"

He was calm, interested, and played along.

"George, of course."

"But who's been making you so miserable for so many years, George or Georgia?"

Because Georgia is in his quality world, I can use that external-control expression. Ordinarily, as you will see when I work, I try not even to intimate that someone else can make us miserable.

"I guess you could say, Georgia. If she weren't there, I could deal okay with George."

"Well, if Georgia's been the one who's been making you so miserable, why kill George? I would think that you'd want to get to know Georgia before you do anything so drastic as killing yourself. Georgia may be a very happy woman. A hell of a lot happier than George is right now."

"You're telling me to go ahead with the operation despite my reservations about my wife."

"If the only alternative is killing yourself, absolutely."

"But what if I don't kill myself and I don't have the operation. What about that?"

With this question, I could lighten the mood of what we were doing.

"My friend, that's where you are right now. If you want to stay that way, it's fine with me. But you better check it out with Georgia; she may have some objections. She very much wants to meet you officially."

I know enough about the quality world to know that if George is a woman in that world, he can never be happy as a man. To counsel him otherwise would be fraudulent. But I also know that there's more to the operation than just getting the surgery. The main reason George wants to kill himself instead of continuing to suffer is that more and more, he's feeling he'll be alone after the operation. I agree with him that his wife's acceptance of the surgery would certainly help. But her acceptance is not crucial to the success of the surgery. Either way, it will be up to him to figure out how to handle her. And he'll also have me to help him through it.

"You talk about Georgia as if she's actually alive."

"You've been breathing her air, and her heart's been pumping your blood. She occupies almost every thought that goes through your head. She's very much alive. But if you want to meet her, to get to know her, to see who might be attracted to her, you've got a lot of work to do even before we worry about how to tell your wife."

"What kind of work?"

"The way I see it is first, you need a lot of information. The place to start is by talking to a doctor who does these operations. Tell him about me and all we've talked about. Surgeons who do these operations are part psychiatrists; they have to be. The first thing to find out after you get to know him is if he'll operate. I don't know much about it, but I'm sure those surgeons don't take everyone who walks in the door. Then if he will take you, ask him if he'll give your name to half a dozen people he's operated on and ask them to get in touch with you. These people may not be able to answer all your questions, but they have a better chance than anyone else. How does this sound to you?"

"The doctor I've heard about is in Portland."

"Go up there and talk to him. He'll talk to you; he'll want to talk to you. Stop moping and go about finding out what you need to know. I'm not just your friend; I'm Georgia's friend, too."

"I wonder why I was so sure you wouldn't accept me."

"Look, I'm here, the gun's here, you're safe for a while. Go talk to the doctor. Do it this week. I'd like you to have something to tell me. Call me as soon as you get back. I'll start thinking about what we can tell your wife."

We'll stop now with George and come back to him when he returns from Portland.

8

Jerry (Continued)

If he breaks out a bar of soap the first time they go to bed, it's all over.

I didn't hear anything from Jerry during the time between then and his next appointment. I was encouraged. If there'd been any trouble, I'm sure he would have called. He was there for his scheduled appointment on Tuesday. As usual he was prompt. He came right in, sat down, and then looked at me as if to show me he could act like a normal person, he had no more difficulty with the lines in my office. It was obvious he was in a great mood; it must have been a good week. I started in by saying, "You seem chipper. What's been going on?"

"Well, I am. And a lot's been going on. I threw a little party at my house and it worked out well.

"That is good news. Who came?"

"Carol, of course, and the couple who lives next door who own the cat. They know all about me. They're not blind; I always use my back-step walk when I go to get my mail out of the box on the street. I've even talked to them about it, we've been neighbors for over twenty years. They told me their cat, Blaze, wants to help me; they encourage him to come over. And by the way, he was at the party, too. I bought him some fresh fish, six bucks a pound, he deserves it. I've been a tough client for him. But I think he's breaking through. But he admits you've done your part, too."

"Do you cook?"

"Of course I cook; I'm not helpless in the kitchen like

Melvin Udall. And I don't have to tell you I've got a very clean kitchen. More and more I've been having Carol over for dinner. She loves my cooking and she's met the neighbors. Okay, I'll admit it, it was her idea to give the party. I could see the surprised look on your face when I told you about it."

"Okay, I'll admit I was surprised."

"But listen, this is the crazy thing that happened halfway through the meal. The food was great, I outdid myself. We were all laughing and joking and then, right in the middle, we'd just finished the main course, I'd say around nine-thirty, I suddenly got up. I mean it was as if I was drawn to do it. I went right to the front door and began to lock it and unlock it, all three locks. I just stood there doing it. You can see the front door from the dining room, and they all just watched me. I guess this went on for two minutes, I was really busy. I mean I hadn't done that now for quite a few weeks, and I'd never done it when anyone was there to see me."

"What do you mean, you haven't done it for a long time? I don't understand."

"Oh, I still go through the routine of locking and relocking but only one or two cycles, that's all. This time was like the old days; I just kept doing it over and over. Can you make any sense out of that?"

"Were you upset, frightened, did you start doing anything else, like getting up to wash your hands? Anything besides the locking and unlocking?"

"No, that was it. I didn't have an urge to do anything else."

"How did you feel while you were doing it?"

"A little foolish, not much else."

"And you did it while you were having a real good time? I mean it wasn't just you. All of you were having a good time."

"Yeah, that's it exactly. We were all having a good time. I mean what I did was from outer space. Why in the hell did I do it? Are things like this just going to keep happening?"

"I hate to sound like a broken record, Jerry, but things like this don't just happen. You choose to do them, you choose everything you do. You were aware of what you were doing."

"Okay, okay, I chose it. But why? I was having such a good time."

"Did it spoil the evening? You're in such a good mood I can't believe it spoiled anything."

"But that's just it. It didn't spoil a thing. I don't think you could guess what happened in a million years. You know what they did while I was standing there running the locks?"

I just looked at him, I hadn't the faintest idea.

"Doc, they got up and came over. Carol grabbed my hand and began to sing that old nursery tune, you know, the one about the mulberry bush. They all joined in, and I joined in too. We began to sing, 'This is the way he locks the door, he locks the door, he locks the door, this is the way he locks the door so early in the morning.' I kept running the locks for about a minute after I started singing, and then I stopped. But I didn't stop singing. I know this sounds crazy but it seemed so funny, we were all laughing our heads off. I guess you had to be there. Then Jack, my neighbor, went over to the piano, he's a musician, he can play any song there is and he kept playing that tune. We kept singing and we went through all my routines. The ones they knew about plus a few they didn't even know I used to do. You know, Doc, it's like a miracle. It's not that I've stopped doing all those things, I still avoid the occasional crack and I still like to keep my hands clean but you know what? I tell myself I'm choosing it and I enjoy it. It's like I've got control over it now. I can't exactly explain it, and I don't care if you can't explain it. I just feel a lot better."

"What did you do after that?"

"Nothing much; we all like music. I got out my guitar and we spent the rest of the evening singing. It was the best night I've had in years. It's all different now. Like the next morning when I went for the paper, I skipped a little and back-stepped a little. The difference was I didn't feel as if I had to do it. When I came back in I ran the locks a few times and sang the song, but the rest of the day I left the door alone. I don't know how to say this, but with Carol my goofy stuff is now an asset. What used to be so screwy is now a lot of fun. Did you see how I walked in today? Just like a regular human being. I thought about coming in singing, 'This is the way I do the cracks, I do the cracks,' but I didn't want you to think I'm crazier than I am. Maybe I'll do it on the way out. But Doc, is this going to last?"

"That's up to you, Jerry. And I guess up to Carol, too. I mean if you two can continue to get along it's a good start, but you still have a way to go. You were a miserable, lonely, angry human being for a long time. If someone would've told you a few weeks ago that Carol and your neighbors would be having dinner with you at your home, and with the cat—well, you know what I'm talking about."

This was the time to do a little explaining, kind of help Jerry put it all together. He had been able to change what he was doing, what he had done for years, because he finally had the support of a person, really people he cared for, if you include his neighbors. And my support, too. Their choice to accept his symptoms and encourage him to make fun of them is what offered him control over them. As long as he has these people in his life, he won't need symptoms anymore. This is why I have to keep seeing him; he still needs help to maintain relationships.

I said, "What have you got, Jerry, that you didn't have before?"

"What do you mean?"

"When did you ever have a good time in your house?"

"I've never had a good time in that house. I haven't had such a good time since."

Then there was a long pause. It was hard for him to admit how bleak his life had been. Immediately, I said, "It really doesn't matter when you last had such a good time. What I'm trying to point out is that when you began to laugh at yourself with your friends, especially with Carol, you didn't need the symptoms. Jerry, you haven't laughed at yourself in years. An old psychiatrist friend told me when I was starting out that when a patient begins to laugh at himself, he's really made progress."

"You don't care much about the past, what happened to me, my life, do you?"

"You know how I feel about it."

"It's okay with me, but I thought all that stuff was important."

"If you think it's important, I'll listen. But don't think I have to know all you've been through; I don't. It was bad enough when it happened. What's the sense of dredging it up again?"

That answer seemed to satisfy him. But then his mood changed, and I could see that something was wrong. And it was. As I looked at him he began to explain.

"Doc, I've got a big problem. I could still screw things up with Carol."

"Do you want to tell me?"

"Okay, no sense beating around the bush, it's sex."

"You've had a problem with sex with her?"

"No, not with her. We haven't had any sex. I haven't pushed for it, and you know what she's been through—no not the details, I don't know those myself, but it was a lot. But in the past few weeks, she seems different. . . . I don't know exactly how to tell you this. You see it's not a problem now but it's going to be, I know it's going to be."

"Do you do anything sexual at all besides what you told me, you hold each other?"

"Sure, we do that all the time, but that's all we do."

"She's said something?"

"No, she hasn't said anything. Last weekend Jill came home, and they spent Saturday night at my house. Separate bedrooms, and then we drove her back on Sunday and she didn't seem to want to leave the car and go into her apartment. Doc, we love being with each other."

There was a long pause.

"But I think I have to make a move, do something, say something that'd tell her I'm interested in sex if she wants it. One of these days she's going to want it. And my problem is I'm not sure I'm ready. I may not be able to do it with her; I might fail. I don't think she realizes this but if it happens . . . Oh God, I'm so worried I'm beside myself. I don't know what to do."

"Do you have any sex at all in your life now?

"I have a woman. She likes me because I'm real clean. I buy her presents, and she likes to hear me play the guitar. She's married. She doesn't depend on me. Maybe once a week, it seems to be all I need. If Carol and I get together, I'll drop her in an instant. But Doc, that woman and I don't really have sex together."

"What do you do?"

"She relieves me with her hands. Believe me, I bring a fresh bar of soap and she has to wash her hands right in front of me. That's all. I don't do anything for her."

"Why does she put up with it? What's in it for her?"

"Like I said, I buy her presents, I talk to her about what I'm writing. She doesn't have much going for her, she doesn't mind doing what I want."

"Have you ever had sex?"

Here I've asked a question about the past. But it's not a fishing trip. It deals with a very important present issue: Has he ever had satisfying sex with a woman he cared for? My guess is he hasn't. But if he has, then that information would make what we have to work on now more hopeful. It's not as if it's hopeless now, but it's going to be more difficult if we're starting from the beginning with a man his age. An analogy would be that a person has been blind all his life and then, as an adult, gets his sight back. He literally has to learn to see, and it takes time. All I can do is help him to see. No matter how dismal a client's past may have been, I can't counsel backwards; no one can change a second of what happened or didn't happen. And it also doesn't matter whose fault it was; that's over too.

"I'm afraid to have sex, it's dirty. I had it three times with prostitutes years ago but I was scared to death I'd catch something. I think that's when I started washing my hands. I love Carol, what can I do? She's been rubbing my back when we hug and last night we had a kiss. Doc, she's a normal woman. I can feel she wants me, and because I've gone so slowly, she has no fear of doing it with me. I mean I don't know that because we've never talked about it but that's the way it seems to me right now. . . . Doc, I'm really scared to death."

"But you've written some romantic movies."

"But that's the catch, what makes them romantic is there's no sex. I mean the characters are going to have it in the end, that's clear. I didn't write them, but they're like the old Doris Day and Rock Hudson movies. You know what I mean. To tell you the truth—God, this is so hard to tell you—I don't know much about sex. I think the first real kiss in my whole life was last night."

I was surprised, not overly surprised, but surprised. To him sex and romance are very loosely connected. What he may be finally ready to do is to connect romance with sex. He hasn't been able to do this so far, but that doesn't mean he can't. This also explains the reason for all his anger. And all his compulsions are his way of dealing with it. He's never had the most basic of all relationships, a good sexual relationship with a woman. For most of his adult life, he's denied he even needed one. That Jack Nicholson movie coupled with meeting Carol has broken through years of denial. But now the idea that he may be inadequate can't be swept under the rug anymore. For Jerry this is put-up or shut-up time. If he doesn't make it with Carol, he'll go back to the way he was, or worse. And if he breaks out a bar of soap the first time they go to bed, it's all over.

I said, "Help me, you know yourself better than anyone knows you. Do you have any idea how to handle this?"

"No, I don't. But I do have some time. I don't think she's in any hurry to go to bed. But I guess there's a limit to how much time."

Then I paused. I didn't know what to tell him. Jerry is looking to get the process started. He needs to take a chance on failing as long as he knows that initial failure is not the end of the world. I'm almost sure that as long as he's tender and loving, Carol will be willing to help him. But like the blind man who unexpectedly regains his sight, the problem is not to get him to see, it's to get him to where he'll try to use his eyes. We both just sat there. After a while I got an idea.

"Jerry, you're right. Sex is going to come up, and I believe you want it to come up. It is what you want, isn't it?

"More than anything I've ever wanted. I'm smart enough to know that wanting it as much as I do is going to make it more difficult, but I can't seem to want it any less."

"Jerry, I've got an idea. You're a successful writer. I'd like you to write something. But just for me, I'll be the only one who'll ever read it unless you decide to show it to someone else."

His face had a puzzled look. I went on.

"I want you to write the end of a story you've never written. A story you may never write. I want you to figure out a romance between two characters, one a rich guy your age and the other a loving younger woman who's been married so she knows about sex. Have them fall in love like you and Carol are doing now. She's had a bad experience with sex in her marriage. She wants you, but she's hoping you can approach her in a way that'll work for her. You're an author. Figure out how to get together sexually, at least get it started. I mean a lot further than you've ever written before."

"But wait a minute—I've never done anything like that."

"But you've written about people in love, you've fantasized about sex. You're fantasizing about it right now all the time. You and Carol are in the position your lovers are in when your stories end?"

"Maybe a little further along."

"That's good. You're at least doing a little more than thinking about it. But because you've never gone as far as you've gone with Carol, does that stop you from writing about it?"

"I write from my imagination. My imagination falls in love all the time."

"That's good; have them head over heels in love. Just take it a step further, not in real life, just on paper. Use your imagination. No one will know. I'll be the only one to read it, and I won't criticize anything you write."

He had that funny look on his face that people get when a new and intriguing idea is slowly registering. I supported it.

"Jerry, I think you can do it. And it's safe. It may give us a start."

"But I'm not so sure I can do it."

"Of course you're not. If you were, you wouldn't have this problem. But good things have already happened that you never believed could happen. What would you have said if I'd told you the last time we met that you were going to give a party and in the middle of it sing that mulberry bush song?"

"Okay, I see what you're driving at. I will. It makes sense."

"Go to work on it. When you finish it, send it to me. Or bring it over. As soon as I read it, we'll get together. Keep seeing Carol, but don't tell her anything about this. You've got time; you said she doesn't act upset at all that you're going slow."

"You don't want to talk about sex, do you? I think I've got the only shrink in the country who won't talk about sex. Are you afraid of it, too?"

"That's good, very good. If you want to, put that in the story too."

When people choose painful or crazy symptoms, it's not because they enjoy them. It's because they don't know anything better to do. Because of his good relationship with Carol, Jerry seems ready to give up his compulsions, even make fun of them a little. But this fear of sex has to do with the fact that he's never allowed himself to have a good sexual relationship with a woman. But that's just what I don't want to talk about. I rarely talk about failures—that makes things worse. Jerry knows what he can't do. My job is to help him move to what he *can* do, or at least imagine that he can.

Reality therapy is a doing method. Of course we talk, but I try to guide people in the direction of actually starting to do something about their problems. In a sense I did the same thing with George. His relationship problem was a lot more severe than Jerry's. But right from the start, I persuaded George to do something: to put his gun in my desk, write the contract, and go see the doctor. It's this attempt at corrective action that is a key factor in the success of reality therapy.

9

Maureen

I'm sure she isn't the only woman in the world who wants to stay married even if her marriage is very bad.

Recently, in Cork, Ireland, while signing books and answering questions after a lecture on choice theory, I had an impromptu therapy session with a middle-aged woman who waited until everyone else had left. I don't know her name, but I'll call her Maureen. She was well dressed, attractive, not slender but certainly not overweight for her age. She seemed a little shy at first, but she quickly became comfortable, and I enjoyed talking with her. She began by saying,

"First of all, I'd like you to sign my book." I did so, and then she said, I wonder if you'd talk to me for a few minutes about my husband?"

"Sure, no problem. I don't have anything scheduled for the next half hour. Everybody's gone; we can just sit here in the front row and talk."

"I guess you gather I've a problem. You talked about how good relationships are necessary for happiness, and my marriage is miserable. I really need some advice. I'm at my wits' end, I don't know what to do."

"Could you tell me what you think is wrong?"

I say, what "you" think is wrong to make sure she knows that I'm aware there are two sides to every marital problem and that all she can tell me is hers. She had no problem with that and went on.

"He doesn't talk to me. He either says nothing or he tells me how much he wants a divorce. He leaves home for days at a time and never tells me where he's gone. If I ask, he says it's none of my business where he goes or what he does. This even happens when we are on vacation. He likes to go to the Canary Islands, but when we're there, he doesn't want me to leave the hotel even though he comes and goes as he pleases. Sometimes he stays away for three days. Even at home he wants me to stay around the house and doesn't give me any more money than to buy the bare necessities, mostly food. Both our children are grown and have left Ireland. I have no friends because he doesn't want me out of the house. And he doesn't want anyone coming to the house.

"Do you have any family around?"

"Just my sister. No one else. She lives close by. He let's her come to the house, but he threatens me with bodily harm if I have any one else over. She's afraid of him. She tells me to give him a divorce, but I don't want to."

"Has he actually struck you?"

"No, not yet, but I feel it could happen at any time?"

I looked for marks or any attempt to cover them up, but I couldn't see anything. I said, "I guess I'm like your sister. I don't understand why you stay with a man who treats you this way. There's divorce in Ireland now, why not take advantage of this opportunity?"

"I don't want a divorce. I want to stay married."

This mind-set seemed strange to me, but I found out by asking my Irish colleagues that this is not an uncommon attitude in Ireland even though divorce is now available. Being a married woman still carries much more status than being divorced. Still, Maureen's choice to stay married in this situation seemed to preclude any possibility of happiness. How could I help her if she wouldn't leave a marriage like this? I felt impotent and said,

"How about him, why doesn't he get a divorce? He could leave you and get it started. From what I understand, that's the way it works here now."

"It's legal, but it's not easy unless I give my consent. He

keeps telling me, we'll divide up all our property and then we should split. He keeps saying, 'I'm miserable being married to you. Why don't you give me a divorce and make it easy on both of us? I don't want to be married to you anymore.' Recently, he's been threatening to kill me if I won't give him a divorce."

"Can't he get one without your consent?"

"He can, but he seems to think it will be a lot easier with my consent. I really don't understand why he just doesn't go ahead without me, but I guess there are a lot of things about him that I don't understand. Maybe my refusal gives him an excuse for all his ranting. This way he can blame me instead of himself. But I won't give him what he wants. I want to stay married, I want to be a married woman. Can't you give me some advice on how to make my marriage better?"

When she asked that question, I was totally frustrated. I'm sure she isn't the only woman in the world who wants to stay married even if her marriage is a disaster. I'd like to give her some advice, but I have no idea what she could do that would make this marriage better.

I said, "When you're home and he's home, how do you act?"

"What do you mean?"

"I mean the expression on your face, your tone of voice, what actually comes out of your mouth, your body language, your whole demeanor. Do you keep sending the message, *I'll never give you a divorce. What I want is a better marriage.* I mean, do you act as if it's all his fault, he has to change?"

"Well, I guess you could say I do because it is all his fault. I'm a good wife, I stay home like he asks me to. I never argue or start a fight. All I ask is that he treat me a little better. I'm getting more afraid of him; he's been threatening me more and more lately."

"This is a hard question, but I want to ask it. If you don't want to answer, it's fine with me. Do you care what he does when he's not with you?"

"Of course I care. I worry all the time if he's going to do something that will disgrace me, disgrace our children, my family."

"Okay, you're worried he'll disgrace you, but suppose he doesn't. He hasn't so far, has he?

"No, whatever he does, it hasn't gotten around as far as I know."

"Do you ever tell him directly how dissatisfied you are, or do you keep your mouth shut and just send the message he's doing wrong, that you're upset with him, that you want him to be different?"

"I am upset. I can't help sending that message. I'm miserable as soon as he walks in the door. I've told you how he is. How could I act any different?"

"Are you prepared to do this for the rest of your life?"

"No, no, I'm not demented. But I still think it could be better. That's why I came to your lecture, that's why I bought your book. I appreciate you taking the time to talk with me."

"I can tell you that as long as you send him that message, that it's all his fault, I don't think you have a chance for a better marriage than you have now. There is also the chance he may kill you. Men in his position do lose control and kill."

"So tell me, what should I do? I'm miserable. That's why I've stayed behind to talk with you."

As you can see, we're talking in circles. She isn't going to change; she wants me to tell her how to change him. It seems that changing him is an impossibility, but there is one chance. I doubt if she'll take it, but it's worth a try.

"Could you possibly accept the fact that he won't change? I mean, he's been this way for years, hasn't he? This isn't something recent, is it?"

"No, it's been this way for ten years, but it's getting worse."

"And you've been sending him that message for ten years?"

She nodded.

"Can you accept the fact that he won't change? I mean, from what you tell me, I don't see much hope for getting him to change."

She didn't answer that question, so I just continued.

"What if there was a possibility of having a better marriage, not love or concern but maybe fewer threats and once in a while you could talk with him and it'd be comfortable? And you might not have to stay home all the time like you do now. Would you be interested?

"What would I have to do?"

"Totally change the way you deal with him."

"What do you mean? I still treat him well. I keep my mouth shut."

"Look, I don't want to upset you, but I have a suggestion. I'm sure it's something you might never have thought of."

I think it is perfectly appropriate for therapists to make suggestions. Most people have quite common problems, in this case a very unhappy marriage, and she is asking for help. To deny her something that might be helpful doesn't make any more sense than to insist that you, the therapist, know what she should do and insist that she do it. A suggestion is therapeutic; an order is not.

"I think you should consider setting him free."

"But I told you, I don't want to give him a divorce."

"No, I don't mean give him a divorce. Just tell him something like this, 'I'm going to stop asking you to change, feel free to do anything you want when you're not home. Stay away as long as you want. Don't feel as if you have to tell me anything about what you're doing or who you're with. Just come home when you want to; you don't have to call.'"

"But I'm married, how could I do that?"

"Maureen, I'm not trying to be a smart aleck, but you're putting up with it now. What you won't be doing if you take my suggestion is continue to send the message it's all his fault. You'll be setting him free mentally if not physically."

I paused for a moment; she was thinking. My suggestion

was totally unexpected. She was trying to come to grips with it. I continued.

"Do you have any say now over anything he does?"

"I try to."

"Is it working?"

She still was having a lot of trouble with my suggestion, but finally she barely admitted, "Not really."

"But that's my whole point. Of course you try. We just talked about that; you try and try, and now he's threatening to kill you. I know what I'm suggesting sounds strange, but it may be a lot better than what you're doing now. For ten years, you've been sending him the message that you don't approve of what he's doing. You want him to change. Are you making things better or worse by what you're doing?"

"Worse, I guess. But I'm not trying to do that."

"I'm not saying you are. I'm saying that that's the way you come across to him. If you keep doing what you're doing, it's almost certain he'll keep doing what he's doing, and it's getting worse. I'm suggesting that you change. Stay married, but give him permission to do what he's going to do anyway. It could make things better; I don't see how it could make things worse. What have you to lose? When he does come home, you may reduce the tension between you, be a little more comfortable together. You could both be happier, and you'll still be a married woman, which is what you say you want. Don't worry about what people will say; no one has to know you set him free except you."

"Are you serious?"

"Can you think of anything better? If he doesn't have to deal with your constant disapproval of all he does or your questioning looks and gestures, his life may be more livable and he may treat you better."

"But he's a married man; I can't just let him do whatever he wants."

"Well, then don't do what I suggest. It's only a suggestion; do whatever you think is best."

There was a long pause in which a thousand years of tradition passed through her mind.

"You're right about one thing: What you suggested would've never crossed my mind. I'll talk to my sister about it. I will. I appreciate you giving me your time."

"You bought the book *Choice Theory;* read it carefully and share it with your sister. Think about it."

She thought about what I said for a few moments. I just looked at her and tried to let her know that I knew what she was struggling with. I knew it wasn't easy. Then she turned and walked out.

Later that day in a seminar with a group of Irish counselors who are practicing and, even teaching, reality therapy and choice theory, I presented what Maureen had discussed with me. I didn't tell them what I suggested—setting him free. I just asked them what they might do with her in this instance. They had a hard time with this question. They were no more separated from tradition than she was. And tradition is external control; it is not choice theory.

I include this session with Maureen to demonstrate that it is a lot easier to talk about giving up external control than it is to do it. External control is so much a part of most people's approach to life that, for a while, the idea of doing something else doesn't occur to them. In this instance, it wasn't so much applying choice theory as getting rid of external-control thinking. Eventually, the counselors got to where my counseling had taken her: set him free. It was an excellent teaching moment.

10

Rebecca

Can you be sane and hear voices at the same time?

When I first saw Rebecca, she was a patient at a local psychiatric hospital. She was twenty-four years old, had been in the hospital for a month, and was diagnosed as suffering from schizophrenia. She was referred to me by her mother, a neighborhood acquaintance. I'd known the family for years. But for the previous ten years, I'd had no contact with any of them.

The mother, Marilyn, was familiar with my work in reality therapy and was dissatisfied with Rebecca's progress. She wondered if the drugs Rebecca had been given were harming her. At each visit she seemed to be getting less emotional—"flat" is how Marilyn described her. I told Marilyn that I was not on the hospital's staff and couldn't see Rebecca as a psychiatrist or do anything about the drug regime. But if Rebecca would like to see me as a visitor, Marilyn could put me on the visitors' list. Rebecca knew who I was and wanted very much to see me. She even showed some positive emotion when her mother brought up the idea. We both thought that was a good sign.

When she first called me, Marilyn told me that Rebecca had been distant, but certainly not separated from the family, since she entered her senior year at the University of California at Santa Barbara. The family kept in touch but were not nearly as close as they'd been previously. Marilyn told me that her daughter had been a whiz in science and math since she was in elementary school and had gone to college to study physics.

The only thing about the college experience that Marilyn

thought might be significant is that Rebecca took an extra year to graduate, telling her family that there was no sense hurrying through. Still she did well in all her classes, and everyone in her highly educated family was pleased when she applied and was accepted to the doctoral program at the same university. Marilyn said that she was puzzled when Rebecca didn't enter graduate school the fall after she graduated college but was pleased that Rebecca had asked for and been given an extension of her acceptance.

About six weeks ago, Rebecca's father died suddenly. Rebecca came home for the funeral and then, to her mother's surprise, decided to stay for a while. She hadn't been home for over a year, even though she lived nearby in Santa Barbara. During the first week she was home, Rebecca told her mother that her admission extension to graduate school had expired but that it was OK because she was still not ready to start the program. She wasn't even sure that physics was what she wanted to study. Marilyn told me that Rebecca seemed surprised when Marilyn didn't make a fuss about the postponement.

When Marilyn asked Rebecca about her life in Santa Barbara and what she planned to do, Rebecca seemed vague. She did mention that she tutored high school and college students in math and physics and had no trouble earning what she needed to support herself.

But by the end of the first week at home, Marilyn felt that something was wrong. Rebecca seemed preoccupied, as if something was on her mind all the time. More and more, she did nothing but listen to music. Even in the middle of the night, Marilyn could hear the music in the den. Finally, Marilyn confronted Rebecca, and Rebecca told her that for the past month, she'd been hearing voices that called her bad names and accused her of disgusting behavior. She couldn't seem to stop the voices, and they were growing louder. When Marilyn suggested that Rebecca needed psychiatric treatment, Rebecca agreed to enter the hospital.

I asked, "Did Rebecca seem upset about her father's

death? I wondered if his death had something to do with the problem. Marilyn said that Rebecca seemed sad but not any sadder than anyone else. But when she thought about it, she said that Rebecca was detached at the funeral—not as involved with the family in the grieving as her mother thought she should have been. When Rebecca decided to stay for a while, Marilyn was very happy to have her; she'd been worried about her even before she came home.

Marilyn had visited Rebecca regularly in the hospital for the month she'd been there. Rebecca seemed satisfied with the hospital routine and told Marilyn that the voices were not nearly as loud or insistent as they had been. However, she complained that the medication made her listless and that she didn't like how it made her feel. Marilyn spoke to Rebecca's psychiatrist about the medication and was told that the flatness was probably caused by the medication but should improve as Rebecca got more used to it.

I asked Marilyn about psychotherapy, but she didn't know much more than that Rebecca was seeing a psychiatric resident every day for a brief conversation and a staff psychiatrist once a week for about twenty minutes. Rebecca was also attending group therapy twice a week but told Marilyn she was not an active participant. Marilyn thought that the medication, plus being in the safe supportive hospital, was the main treatment.

While the voices were diminishing, Rebecca told her mother they were still there. What concerned Marilyn was that Rebecca seemed sad and didn't welcome visits from family members whom she used to be close to. Marilyn told me, "I don't think she's suicidal, but she seems to have lost interest in life.

Marilyn made arrangements for me to visit, and, as soon as I came, Rebecca asked if it would be okay for us to take a walk, rather than to stay in the hospital. She already had privileges to walk on the grounds, and that's what she'd like to do. I had known her through my children when she was in nursery school and elementary school, but we'd had little contact once she left elementary school. We had really never talked; she was just one of the many children in the neighborhood.

The first thing Rebecca said was, "I'm glad to see you," and then we made some getting-reacquainted small talk. Then I asked her if she was talking to a psychiatrist in the hospital.

"I see a psychiatric resident every day. But he seems more interested in how I'm doing on the medication and if I'm hearing the voices less than talking to me about my life. I keep telling him that I don't like the medication, but I have to admit that the voices are less intrusive than before I came here. I also see a staff psychiatrist, but all he wants to talk about is my father's death. I keep telling him that I was this way before my father died, but he keeps probing that event. As far as I can tell, the relationship between my dad and me was good. All the relationships in my home growing up were good. My father's death didn't cause me to be the way I am."

I didn't push for anything more, although I made a mental note to try to find out what she meant when she said, "the way I am." It sounded more significant than just hearing the voices. We just walked, and Rebecca asked me about my life and my children, whom she'd known while she was growing up. She seemed a little flat, but I didn't know what to compare it with, since I hadn't seen her for such a long time. The good part is that she seemed comfortable talking with me. I asked her a little about her friends, and she said she had some friends but no one close. I didn't pursue this matter because we hadn't yet gotten to know each other well enough for me to probe in this area. I had the feeling then, and it has since proved to be the case since I still hear from her, that she was not interested in sexual involvement. Some people are not, and I think she was one of them. What we had was a good-getting acquainted time, and Rebecca seemed to enjoy it. She then asked,

"Don't you want to hear about the voices? They're better now, but they were pretty frightening when they started."

"Do you want to tell me about them?"

"Not particularly. I just thought that's the kind of stuff

you'd be interested in. The resident asks me every time he runs into me. He seems happy that they're better."

She'd brought up the voices for a reason, and I couldn't ignore it. So I asked her a question that I usually ask people with her diagnosis, most of whom are able to talk quite sanely to a therapist they trust. I asked this question matter-of-factly as if I just wanted her opinion on the subject.

"Do you think you're crazy?"

Like almost all the patients I've asked this question, Rebecca didn't take it as an affront. She said, in a kind of sad voice, "I don't know. When I first began to hear the voices, I thought so but now I'm not so sure. Can you be sane and hear voices at the same time?"

"That's a good question. I guess it depends on how much you believe they're actually there. As long as you recognize they're not coming from real people, they're coming from your head. And if you seem to have a good grasp of reality, which it seems to me you have, I think you can be sane and hear voices at the same time. Did you want to come to the hospital, or are you here because your mother wanted you to come?"

"No, I wanted to come. But I thought it would be different."

"In what way?"

"I don't know, maybe they'd be a little more interested in me. I mean not so interested in the voices or in my father's death or in my career that's never happened . . . interested in what I'm doing now with my life. I mean me, like what I want."

That's the problem of being diagnosed with a mental illness, especially with the illness called schizophrenia. With the advent of psychiatric medication, it's treated as if there's something wrong with her brain that must be corrected by drugs, as if the way she was choosing to live her life and satisfy her needs didn't have much to do with what's happening in her head. Medication is very popular because it takes the problem from the psychological, which seems so hard to grasp, to the physical, which is tangible. And family members are reassured that they didn't do anything wrong. It's an illness, and there are drugs to cure it. I'm not saying that drugs are never indicated, but right now they're used too much. And psychotherapy, which used to be a major psychiatric skill, more and more is taking a backseat to drugs. Almost all the psychotherapy today is done by nonpsychiatric professionals, such as psychologists, who cannot prescribe medication. But psychologists are now pushing for the privilege to prescribe. If they get it, psychotherapy will take another hit. I then responded to Rebecca's last statement.

"Tell me, what do you want?"

I'm trying to find out what's in her quality world. I know from choice theory that there's something in that world that's frustrating her severely. It's probably a conflict; she's in what's been called a double bind. It's like coming to a fork in the road and wanting to take off in both directions or neither direction but having to keep going. I don't know the exact situation, but I'm sure she'll tell me. It's very much on her mind.

"I'm not sure. I think I know, but I'm not at all sure."

That answer didn't surprise me. Psychiatrists have believed for years that psychotic symptoms in young adults, like the voices Rebecca was hearing, are related to young adults' concern about their future. Especially, in young people who seemed for a long time to be successful and goal oriented. I believe that the symptoms are their way of choosing to avoid facing the future. What they should do with their lives may be clear in the minds of their family—in Rebecca's case to pursue a career in physics. But it isn't nearly as clear in their minds, and they have trouble with this probing question. I continued to try to find out what was wrong, what relationship Rebecca was concerned about.

"Is it that you think you should know what you want?"

When I asked that question, Rebecca seemed to perk up and looked right at me for the first time. It was important to her that she talk about what she wants, and she wanted to talk about her future. But I also felt that she didn't want me to tell her what to do with her life; she'd had plenty of advice on that issue.

"I'm twenty-four years old. I've finished college. Don't you think I should know what I want?"

"Rebecca, I don't think it's unusual that you haven't made up your mind. What's the hurry? You're supporting yourself. Give yourself some time."

"That's what I've been telling myself, but how much time? Don't you think I should put all the education I've had to use in my life?"

I saw this question as a test. Rebecca was trying to find out if I was biased toward her going on in physics. Or if had an open mind and would accept the fact that she didn't want to pursue a career in physics right now. Maybe never. I said,

"Well, this much I know. . . . Right now, you're not looking for a career in physics or math. You'd have no trouble doing the work, but you've let the doctorate go."

She tested a little more.

"Why do you say that? I'm good in physics and math. I could reapply any time."

"I'm sure you could. And I'm also sure you'd be accepted. But I don't believe you'd be in this hospital hearing voices if you were set on that career."

"What do you mean?"

"Because you're in a bind. People who suddenly hear voices are struggling with a problem. It's often a problem about their future—a kind of struggle between what they want to do and what they think they should do. Do you think that part of you wants to be a physicist but there's also a big part of you that wants to do something else with your life? Maybe you were even doing it in Santa Barbara this past year. I don't know."

"You sound so sure of that. I'm not so sure that's the problem at all."

"I don't deny that I'm guessing. But a lot of experience with young people like you tells me that's what's likely going on."

"Well it is; you're right."

"Tell me why're you having so much trouble giving up on physics, at least for now. Is anyone putting pressure on you?

"There's been pressure on me for a career in science since I was in grade school. But it wasn't my parents. Well, I'm not so sure. I guess there was some pressure but nothing severe. It was just taken for granted that's what I'd do. And after I did so well in college that take physics-for-granted pressure increased. But it wasn't only my parents, it was also from my teachers and my close relatives. I thought I was headed in that direction when I graduated. Then, all of a sudden, it wasn't what I wanted to do. I don't want to go to graduate school right now. I've found a good life in Santa Barbara, but I can't seem to let myself live it."

There's more here than the obvious external pressure. That's the easy answer, but I don't think it's the only answer.

"I'm interested. Tell me some more about this good life. I'm trying to help you figure out what's best for you. Forget what you think you should do. Let the future go for a while and tell me what you enjoy doing right now."

In reality therapy, we try to focus on the present situation with which clients are struggling. To push into the future until the present is under control could be a mistake.

"I want to do what I've been doing in Santa Barbara. I'm happy with my life there. But I can't help thinking, *I'm letting the people who love me down.*"

"Have any of them been pressuring you recently to go ahead with graduate school?"

"No, not at all. Sure, my mother's a little disappointed if you could call that pressure, but that's all; she's made no direct efforts to get me to go on in physics. You know her, she isn't that kind of person. . . . But you know what? I've kind of taken over for the rest of them. It's me; I'm pressuring myself."

That's what makes a conflict like this so difficult. You can get away from the pressure of other people, but you can't get away from the pressure you put on yourself. I didn't say anything, and Rebecca thought for a long time.

Finally, she said, "That's right, It's not her; it's not anyone.

As the time went on and I let physics go, more and more I've been pressuring myself."

"What do you mean?"

"I can't help thinking I'm selfish. I should consider how my family feels. Even my dad, he never pressured me, but he made it clear he had a vision of me being a scientist. He didn't criticize me, but about a year ago, when I was home for a few days, we talked quite a bit about it. . . . It's just hard for me to accept what I'm doing now. It's so unimportant, but it's the life I want."

"Tell me about it?"

"First of all, I support myself. I make money, good money, tutoring kids. I mean high school kids and college kids from rich families. Santa Barbara is loaded with those kids. It's funny, even though I don't want a career in math or physics, I do enjoy tutoring those subjects. . . . I guess, what I really enjoy is the kids; I like to see their excitement when I teach them something that really hits home. And I'm in demand; I could have twice as many students if I wanted. Tuesday, Wednesday, Thursday, that's all I tutor.

I knew there must be more; I just kept looking at her. Finally Rebecca admitted what was bothering her, what she really meant when she said, "It's so unimportant."

"Ever since I was small, I've liked to play games. I waited to grow out of it, but I haven't. What I really enjoy doing is playing duplicate bridge and chess. They're very different, but I love them both. And even cribbage. Cribbage is all about probability, like modern physics. I play cribbage with my math pupils; it gives them a real math experience. And I also like crossword puzzles. . . . But I don't like to gamble. I love games and I'm good at them, but I have no interest in winning money. The woman whose guest house I live in introduced me to bridge, and now she's my partner. We've already won a lot of points. We go out of town to tournaments. She's got money; it's all first class, and we've come close to winning a big one. And I love listening to music. I've got a new CD player and wonderful speakers. I tutored day and night for a while to get that setup. I like to listen to it at night and then be able to sleep in the morning. I love having mornings with nothing to do."

"Is it too good a life for you to accept?"

"That's a good way of putting it. I'm okay until I come down to LA. I may be wrong, but I don't think that what I'm doing in Santa Barbara is acceptable here. So I procrastinate about coming down, and that becomes a problem, like I should go and visit. . . . But I don't want to. . . . You really think the way I'm living up there has something to do with my hearing voices?"

"I think so; I think they're connected. But look, you're a game player; you like to solve problems. When you're playing chess, does a great new move, even a move that's in the future, suddenly pop into your mind? A move totally different from what you were thinking about, maybe different from what you've ever used before?"

"All the time. It happens in bridge, too."

"In the next three days before I can see you again, I'd like you to think about how new ideas pop into your mind. . . . And maybe also think about how you're pressuring yourself to give up a life you want to lead. . . . Is Friday this time, okay?"

I didn't want to answer Rebecca's question about the voices in too much detail. I just said, "I think they're connected." I wasn't ready to deal with that possible connection before we had gotten to know and, I hope, trust each other better. But I did want to give her those things to think about. I'm sure she will.

I believe that the conflict between what she wants to do and what she thinks she should do has everything to do with the voices she's been *creating in her brain*. To explain this belief, I have to introduce another component of total behavior that may be both causing the voices and popping creative chess and bridge moves into her mind. Total behavior almost always has a creative component. It is even hard to do a routine task over and over without getting the idea, *I can do this better*. Here I'd like to explain human creativity or, to be more specific, total behavioral creativity.

For example, if our total behavior is made up of four distinct but inseparable components—*acting, thinking, feeling,* and *physiology*—each component has a separate capacity to be creative. But because all the components are linked, any time one or more of the four becomes creative, the result is a new total behavior based on the axiom: *If you change any part, you change the whole.*

I will not attempt to explain human physiological creativity; it is too speculative and complicated for this book. (I cover it in detail in Chapter Seven of *Choice Theory*.) Here I focus on creative actions, thoughts, and feelings that play such an important role in both our waking and sleeping lives.

We see creative *acting* whenever we watch professional athletes, dancers, and actors perform. For example, Michael Jordan creating a new basketball maneuver or Mikhail Baryshnikov creating a new dance movement. Every great actor and actress creates new facial expressions, hand movements, and voice timbre each time he or she performs. Creative thinking has led to millions of scientific discoveries and artistic triumphs. Creative feelings are at the heart of every great performance.

But you don't have to be great or successful to be creative. Creative thinking and feelings, especially those that express misery, are hardly limited to the stage and screen. People who have thought, acted, and felt creatively fill our courtrooms and are frequently seen in our homes and workplaces. They are by far the reason people go to counseling or, in Rebecca's case, to a mental hospital.

So far in this book, I have dealt with a lot of creative total behaviors. For example, Jerry created his obsessions and compulsions and Chelsea created her panic attacks in their own brains. They didn't learn these behaviors from anyone else. Rebecca created the most puzzling total behavior when she created voices that spoke to her from her own brain. But as much as the voices seem real to her, they are no more real than our most common mental perceptual creations: our dreams. Delusions, or strong false beliefs, are in the same genre.

When we create hallucinations or delusions, we are uniformly labeled mentally ill. But when Albert Einstein or Pablo Picasso created new thinking, no one labeled them mentally ill. That label is a subjective psychiatric conclusion: *mentally ill or crazy if it's bad creativity, genius if its good creativity.* Psychiatrists and judges decide what's good and bad.

Most of our creative thinking occurs in the frontal lobe of the brain. If this lobe is cut away from the rest of the brain through a lobotomy or paralyzed with strong psychiatric drugs, people lose most, if not all, their creativity. In suffering this loss, they usually lose the ability to create delusions and hallucinations. But they also lose their ability to create what Rebecca prized so much: creative solutions to bridge and chess problems.

When the frontal lobe is disabled, all creativity is impaired, not just what we consider to be undesirable, such as hallucinations and delusions. For example, we lose the ability to create expressions on our face, which grows masklike and inexpressive. We lose the ability to walk smoothly and gracefully, similar to what happens specifically in Parkinson's disease. And we lose the ability to think spontaneously and quickly. It's as if much of what we need to enjoy life has been taken from our brain.

But with this loss of pleasure, we also lose much of our ability to feel psychological pain, the pain that tells us that our psychological needs—love, power, freedom, and fun—are unsatisfied. What we don't lose is our concern about *survival.* It still feels good to eat and sleep, and we retain the ability to feel hunger and fatigue. This more primitive pain is a product of an ancient vegetative part of our brain. Our more creative thinking and feeling occur in the frontal lobe.

With the loss of psychological pain, we have little interest in trying to satisfy our needs through seeing family, making friends, gaining respect, socializing, or having fun. Without a well-functioning frontal lobe, we become like zombies, alive but quiet. Unfortunately, the psychiatric thinking of the past two centuries is that being quiet and peaceful is a vital component of sanity. Read or reread the book *One Flew Over the Cuckoo's Nest* if you want to refresh your mind about what I am trying to explain here.

People like Rebecca, who are now labeled schizophrenic because of the voices they create, are almost always treated with frontal lobe-disabling drugs that work by paralyzing their creativity. Although in sufficient doses these psychiatric drugs will put a stop to Rebecca's ability to create the voices, they do not act selectively on the voices alone. For a creative game player like Rebecca, this loss of creativity is painful; that's what she was complaining about to her mother that led Marilyn to call me.

But if Rebecca stays on the drugs too long, she may stop complaining because she has lost her desire to satisfy her psychological needs. Winning, a power need, will no longer be important to her. I was pleased that Rebecca complained about the drugs, that she was not yet at the point where she didn't care if her needs were satisfied or not. She wasn't crazy in the sense that, almost from the beginning, she knew the voices were hallucinations. But someone a lot more psychotic than Rebecca would not know this fact, and the drugs would have been given in larger doses and for a longer time. And the longer that people are on these drugs, the less they want to do to satisfy their needs. And the less they want to satisfy their needs, the less effective is psychotherapy.

Contrary to much current thinking, there is no problem doing psychotherapy with a person who hears voices or suffers from delusions. Although I accept that the symptoms are there, I rarely refer to them in therapy. Most psychotic people can be reached if you concentrate on what they do that is sane. Which is much of what they do all day: eat, sleep, bathe, watch TV, read, and talk to staff and other patients. I focus on these sane behaviors and work hard to try to create what I know every client I have ever seen, psychotic or not, wants: *good relationships that start with me.*

Rebecca is fearful that the life she is choosing to lead in Santa Barbara will alienate her from her mother and family. This fear, coupled with all the pressure she is putting on herself to give up that satisfying life, is triggering her creativity to produce the voices. My task is to create a good-enough relationship with her so that I can encourage her to live the life she wants. She no longer receives much pressure from her family; it's the pressure she puts on herself that's the problem.

It is important to understand that all the creative system can do is create and that a lot of our creativity may have nothing to do with reducing frustration. Basically, every total behavior we choose has a creative component. What we learn to do as we live our lives is accept helpful creativity and attempt to reject worthless or destructive creativity. But we can't just choose to reject a hallucination. To get rid of it, we have to figure out ways to satisfy one or more of our basic needs better than we can at the time our creativity offers us the hallucination.

But hearing the voices did persuade Rebecca that she was having difficulty living the life she wanted, so she went home, told her mother, and got help for the conflict that activated her creative system to produce the voices. As painful, crazy, or disabling as these symptoms are, all symptoms are creative to some extent—and hallucinations to a large extent. But whatever the symptom is, from the most common symptom, depressing, to obsessing, compulsing, panicking, and psychosing and all the other symptoms defined as mental illness, it is created for the following three reasons:

1. The symptom helps us to restrain the anger that is always present whenever we are frustrated. As angry as Jerry was, he might have been much angrier if he didn't devote so much time and energy to his obsessions and compulsions. If George hadn't depressed so strongly, he might have turned his anger against himself and committed suicide; he came dangerously close. Unchecked anger is dangerous, as

can be seen in parts of cities where anger often goes unchecked or in parts of the world where murder is the solution to all political conflicts. And for very angry people, life is cheap.

2. The symptom is a cry for help. Choosing to depress is by far the most frequent way we do so, but every symptom that restrains anger can be seen as a cry for help. It is almost impossible to see another human being depressing and not offer some assistance.

3. We use symptoms to avoid situations that we fear will increase our frustration. Many people depress after losing a job. When someone tells them to get going, start looking for work, they say, "You're right I should, but I'm just too depressed." The choice to depress gets them off the hook for a while. What they are afraid of is further rejection. Painful as depressing is, it is less painful than facing this possibility.

All symptoms help us gain more control over the situation. For Rebecca, the voices certainly restrained any anger she might have felt from family pressures. They also were a successful cry for help: She and her mother got reconnected because of them, a connection she feared she might have been losing. The third reason didn't apply. She wasn't afraid of college; she just didn't want to make science her life.

There is also a huge group of people who, when they are unable to satisfy their needs, are able to restrain their anger and call for help by creating a physical symptom. What they mostly create are a variety of aches, pains, fatigue, and other physical symptoms like allergic conditions for which no doctor can find a medical cause. But unlike creating voices, panicking, or obsessing, aches and pains are not usually considered psychological problems.

As long as people have medical insurance, almost every such

complaint is exhaustively investigated at a huge expense. And even though no physical source of the pain can be found, patients and even some physicians refuse to believe that this suffering has been created in the patients' brains. The only way to find out is to try psychotherapy in addition to whatever medical treatment may still be indicated. This refusal to believe, shared by both patients and physicians, costs billions of dollars each year in expensive diagnostic procedures, such as MRIs.

I am not saying that these complaints should be ignored, but there should be a limit to what is done without concurrently offering some counseling. If both patients and the physicians who treat them could learn that when we are frustrated, we are able to create almost any action, thought, feeling, or physiology our brain is capable of experiencing, we could save huge amounts of physicians' time and effort. And relieve a great deal of suffering in the process.

Once symptoms are created, we are able to choose to employ this creativity again and again with little effort. For example, if Rebecca is unable to satisfy the pictures of game playing in her quality world, it will be easy for her to start hallucinating again. Once a person's brain creates a headache or backache, he or she can keep creating it even if there is no physical cause for the pain.

On Friday, Rebecca seemed glad to see me. She wanted to take a walk in the neighborhood around the hospital, and we headed in that direction. Along the way she said,

"I don't want to take the medication anymore. The voices have almost stopped, but it feels as if my brain is in a straitjacket. Do you think I still have to take them?"

"I have to be truthful with you. I wouldn't have prescribed these medications to a person like you who didn't have any other signs of craziness other than hearing voices. I'd get to know you first. But I wasn't here when you checked in. You may have been a lot worse then than you were by the time I first saw you. Were you so out of it you couldn't talk sensibly or didn't know where you were?"

"I didn't like the voices, but in a week I figured out they were hallucinations. I knew no one was out there (she gestured with her arm to the area around her) talking to me. It didn't seem as if I was crazy, but I did hear the voices; they had gotten pretty loud and abusive."

"Have you brought up the subject of reducing your medication? Maybe, tell your doctor the voices are almost gone and the medicine is uncomfortable."

"I thought about doing that, but I wanted to check with you first."

"I think it would be okay to ask."

We continued to walk, and she didn't say anything else for a while. I didn't feel uncomfortable with her silence, and she seemed relaxed. Then, as we approached the end of our walk, she brought up the fact that every patient in the hospital whom she talked with was on some sort of medication. She also said that she couldn't figure out why some of them were in the hospital; they never said or did anything crazy. But I assured her that there was a good reason for them to be there. In the safe, supportive hospital environment, it is not unusual for patients to stop creating symptoms. The fact that most patients were on medication is the usual treatment, and it does do some good. But it should not replace psychotherapy, which is usually very effective in helping patients deal with their problems. It was a warm day, and by the time we got back to the hospital, I was ready to sit down.

Then I said, "I don't know if they told you, but the medication is supposed to make it impossible for your brain to create the voices you've been hearing. This may have something to do with the fact that you no longer hear them."

"They did tell me that the drugs can get rid of the voices, but they didn't tell me that my brain was creating them. They said I have a mental illness, schizophrenia. The voices go with the illness."

"Do you feel mentally ill right now? Like you're disoriented or that people are out to get you, any of those things?"

"No, but I think I did at the beginning. The voices kept on day and night, and they wouldn't go away. I mean, I knew where I was, but it was real bad."

"Are you comfortable in the hospital?"

"Now I am. It's pretty good. If you want to have nothing to do, this is a good place to do it."

"But if you stop hearing the voices, they're going to let you go pretty soon. Is that okay with you?"

"It's okay. I want to get back to Santa Barbara. I have a life up there. My mom told me she'll pay my rent while I'm here, but I don't know if my bridge partner will let her; she doesn't need the money. But it's good that I'll have my place to go back to. And I can always get students; I'm a good tutor. . . . I miss my chess games. No one in this hospital plays chess. And I really miss bridge."

"Are you okay with putting your doctorate on the back burner and not pressuring yourself to do what you don't want to do?"

"Yeah, the last time we talked and I got the idea I was pressuring myself, that helped. For the time being, I can just pick up where I left off. To tell you the truth, I never wanted a career in physics, but it's like I got stuck. Once I started down the road to a doctorate, I couldn't seem to get off. And I did like the teachers and the courses. But I also liked it when you said, 'Tell all that stuff to me. You don't need to tell it to anyone else.' But I told my Mom, and she said, 'Fine. Do what you want with your life. There's nothing wrong with what you're doing. I kind of envy you; it sounds like a good life.'"

"Rebecca, my guess, and it's just a guess, is that the voices were trying to tell you: *Relax and live the life you want to*. They were criticizing you and calling you names to remind you to stop trying to do what you don't want to do. Remember, they were your voices; you might not have liked them or what they said, but, in a sense, they were on your side."

"I don't know. I think it's easier to think I was crazy for a while and now I'm over it."

Whether she believes what I suggested is not important. She's on the right track; that's what's important.

"How did you feel when your mother said, 'Do what you want with your life?'"

"It felt real good."

"Good enough so you can stop pressuring yourself?"

"I think so. This whole experience—seeing you, telling my mother about the voices, coming here to the hospital, and her not falling apart—has helped me to understand how much I like the life I'm living up there. And no one's putting any pressure on me to live a different life. You think I can go back up there and get my life going again, don't you?"

"I do. I can't think of anything better for you to do right now."

"But there's one good thing: I got reacquainted with my mom. I'd been avoiding coming home. Like I said, I guess I saw just coming into that house as pressure. Now I think I'll take the bus down every two months or so. I might invite my mom up. That place I'm in has plenty of room. When my dad died, I was really more worried about her than I was about myself. Maybe the voices were trying to tell me to go home, that my mom missed me. I don't know."

I saw Rebecca four more times, and there wasn't much more to say. She was very intelligent, so I did explain that what she evidently needed was support from her mother, even more so because her father was gone. The doctor cut down her medication and then stopped it when she left. I've followed her for the past fifteen years, and the voices have never come back.

Now she reads all my books when they come out. She just dropped me a note telling me how much more she understood about herself after reading *Choice Theory*. I've had quite a few other young clients who are trying to deal with the issues of self and family pressure, and they have all worked out well.

11

TERESA

Teresa, face it. Good or bad, happy or sad, you're choosing everything you do all day long.

On one of the weekly afternoons I volunteered at a family service agency, I was asked to see Teresa. She was forty years old, neat, clean, and attractive despite the fact that she was at least sixty pounds overweight. What impressed me when she came in was her total lack of energy, as if the act of coming to see me was an overwhelming effort. Teresa appeared about as "depressed" as any woman I've ever seen. From my experience with many women like Teresa, I knew that right from the start, I had to avoid getting trapped into what I was sure would be a story of rejection, self-pity, and hopelessness.

I was determined not to ask Teresa to tell me her story and, especially, not to ask her how she felt. I had to try to convince her that she was making ineffective choices in her life, knowing full well that my claim that she was making choices, especially choosing to depress, would be the furthest thing from her mind. If I couldn't begin to convince her on her first visit, there was little chance of any measurable progress.

I started by rising briskly, greeting her warmly, and offering my hand. Teresa was surprised by my energy and enthusiasm to see her. I was not the first therapist she had seen, and she was used to using her depressing to take over the interview and, if she could, immediately strip it of all hope. With a puzzled look on her face, she shook my hand limply and then sat down and just looked at me.

I started by saying in as upbeat a voice as I could muster, "I'm glad you're here. Did you have any trouble getting an appointment?"

I could see that she didn't expect that question. She expected to tell me her tale of woe with many insertions of how awful she felt. It took her a while to shift gears, but I just smiled and waited.

"No, not really. I had to wait for three weeks, but Janet, you know, my social worker, told me it wouldn't be any longer."

I knew Janet. When she asked me to see her she told me Teresa was very depressed. Janet was at her wits' end to know what to do with her. She wanted to tell me more, but she knew me well enough to know that I don't want any history or information about the people I see before I see them. Janet is trying to learn choice theory, but the idea that we choose all we do is a struggle for her.

I continued in my polite upbeat manner, "Was Janet polite to you when she talked to you about seeing me? Is she usually considerate when she sees you?"

Teresa didn't say anything; she just nodded. I knew Janet was always kind and considerate, or I wouldn't have asked that question. But from Teresa's standpoint, it was an unusual show of interest on my part, and I could see her brighten perceptibly.

I continued, "I know you've been here only a moment, but do I seem polite and concerned so far?"

This question may sound like I was going too far, but I was sincere and she accepted my sincerity.

"Yes, you seem fine."

Now I had her attention. Her depressing was diminishing in front of my eyes.

"Teresa, therapy is not easy. I have to ask you some hard questions that may even confuse you a little, but I'm doing it because I want very much to help you. But please, if I say anything that you don't think is right, ask me why, and I'll explain as well as I can. This really isn't a hard question, but I'd like you to try to do your best to answer it. What do you think a psychiatrist can do for you?"

I want her to have some expectations. Not just to sit there and accept that not much can be done. This question will help her to learn that everything we do is important. That if she works with me, she can get some help. She answered as I thought she would; that was what was important.

"Help me to feel better. I feel so depressed. I have no energy. My life is a disaster. Look at me, the only thing I enjoy is eating."

"Fine, that's the answer I was hoping for: You think you can use some help; you haven't given up."

I reframed her hopeless answer into a hopeful one. Teresa ratcheted up her interest another notch, and I continued.

"Now I'm going to ask you a question that may not make much sense. Are you willing to try to answer it?"

"You're the doctor, ask me, and I'll try to answer."

"Is it okay if we don't talk at all about how you feel or about your life. You said it was a disaster; I'd just as leave not talk about it."

"I don't understand. When I've talked to other therapists, that's all they want to talk about. That's what I've been telling Janet; I thought that's why she sent me to you. My God, with a life like mine, what else is there to talk about?"

"Please, Teresa, tell me. Has it done any good to talk about your misery to anyone? Like, do you choose to feel better after telling someone how miserable you are?"

I'm tangentially introducing the idea that she can choose to feel better. I wonder if she'll pick up on it? She didn't.

"Wait a second, you're getting me confused. I've got to tell you how I feel. How can you help me if you don't know how I feel?"

"Teresa, you don't have to tell me how you feel. I know how you feel. Janet knows how you feel. I'm sure everyone you know, knows how you feel."

Now I'll come right out with the idea that she's choosing how she feels; she won't be able to miss it this time.

"Everyone who comes in here is choosing to feel bad. No one who chooses to feel good ever comes in. At least they've never come to see me. I don't think it's a very good choice. That's why I don't want to talk about it."

"I don't know what you're talking about. I don't choose to feel bad."

"Well, if you don't choose to feel bad, then how come you feel bad?"

"I feel bad because my life is a disaster. What else could I feel."

"But does choosing to feel bad help you in any way to feel better? I realize I'm confusing you, but I'm trying to help you. How you feel is a part of the way you choose to live your life. You chose what you did all day yesterday. Did you feel good or bad yesterday?"

I use this technique of looking at yesterday a lot with clients like Teresa who think that at forty years old, they are already doomed to a life of misery. If we look at her life as a whole so far, it probably is hopeless. But if we look back only as far as yesterday, there's a lot of hope. Hope is what I'm working toward. Teresa then gave me the standard answer that too many people who are choosing to depress believe.

"But doctors, several doctors, have told me I'm suffering from depression, clinical depression they called it. It's a mental illness. I can't just choose not to be depressed. . . . Are you really a psychiatrist?"

"Have any of the psychiatrists who've told you you're mentally ill talked to you and helped you?"

"They gave me medication. It helped me feel better for a while, but it doesn't seem to work anymore. That's why I asked Janet if I could see you."

Medication for "depression," which does make people feel better, works best with people who have much more going for them in their lives than Teresa has. But in my experience, therapy works as well or better with these same people.

"I don't plan to offer you medication. I want to talk with you. I want to help you to make better choices in your life, starting right now. Has anyone ever talked to you about the choices you make like I'm doing now?"

"No, not really. Mostly they talk about my problems. What I'm doing with my kids, how I budget my money, my weight, things like that. But I don't think anyone has ever mentioned choices; you're the first one to talk like this."

"Okay, tell me. How do you feel right now? I mean this minute."

"I feel a little angry. I think you're playing games with me."

At this point I got very serious. She could see how important what we were talking about was to me.

"Is feeling a little angry better than how you felt when you walked in? Think about how you feel now and how you felt a few minutes ago when you walked in the door. Let's say hello again. Here, give my hand a good shake."

I reach out my hand, and she gives it a much more vigorous shake than she did when she came in.

"Okay, you're right. I feel a little better. I do."

"Aren't you choosing to feel better? You could have chosen to continue to feel the way you did when you came in. If you were suffering from clinical depression, how could you feel better all of a sudden?"

"I don't know; I don't feel bad all the time. Besides, I don't want to feel bad. I feel better with you."

"I hate to belabor the point, but you chose to stop feeling bad. And you're choosing to feel better with me."

"Okay, I'm choosing to feel better for a few minutes. What good is that going to do me for the rest of my life?"

"Would you like to stop choosing to feel better and go back to choosing to feel bad? You can do it right now if you want to. I believe you're an expert at choosing to feel bad."

"Oh, so you claim all I have to do the rest of my life is choose to feel good, and everything'll be fine? Are you kidding?"

"Okay, it may seem that I am, but I'm not. Follow along with me. I said some of these questions would be puzzling. Tell me why are you choosing to feel a little better right now?"

"I don't know. Maybe because you got me thinking a little. I'd about given up on thinking."

"I got the impression that you'd about given up on everything."

"You can say that again."

"When you give up on your life, what is it that you really give up on? Think a minute. If you can answer that question, I think you can really get some help."

"But if I can't answer it, I can't get any help?"

"Oh my goodness, no. I'll help you answer it. But don't be surprised if you find it hard to answer. I don't think very many people can answer it. It may help if you think about the way you've chosen to be for the past two years since you've been coming to this agency."

She just looked at me. She didn't know what to say, so I continued.

"What changed in your life? You haven't been this way for your whole life."

"Before my husband walked out on me, I felt pretty good. I haven't felt that way for a long time."

"When you felt good, what did you choose to do that you've totally stopped doing now?"

"I did things, I saw people, I took good care of my children, I wasn't broke all the time. I had a life."

"That's a perfect answer except for one little detail. You chose all those good things; you chose to have a life."

"Okay, okay, but that's all gone. In your words, tell me how I can choose to have a life now."

"The same way you chose it then."

"But I had a marriage, I was somebody. I'm nobody now.

Just a poor woman with kids on welfare, and they're going to take that away in a year."

"I'll admit your life was a lot better than it is now, but you're still alive. And if you're still alive, you can still choose to have a life. The only person who can stop you from making better choices right now is you. As long as you choose to depress, you no longer have a life."

"But what else can I choose? I just can't go home and choose to be happy."

"That's right, you can't separate choosing how you feel from choosing what you do. They go together. But you can go home and spend the rest of the day saying to yourself: *Teresa, face it. Good or bad, happy or sad, you're choosing everything you do all day long.*"

I didn't explain total behavior to Teresa, but this is connecting acting to feeling. It worked. She caught on.

"But what difference will that make? I'll still have the same lousy life."

"What do you choose to do all day that keeps your life the same?"

"I sit home, watch my soaps, and eat. That's what I do. That's what a lot of women like me do. I know quite a few of them from the neighborhood. Most of them are just like me. Too old for love, too young to die."

"But not too old to start making some better choices."

"OK, like what?

In print that "like what" seems cynical, but it didn't come out that way at all. She really wanted to know.

"All right, let's start with one. What could you choose to do tomorrow that would be better than today?"

"I could choose not to sit around all day."

"No, that won't work. It'd be like trying to choose not to eat so much. I'm not looking for you to choose *not* to do anything. I'm looking for you to start to choose to do something better than you're doing now. Something active, so that you have to get up and get going."

Then she said something that made us both smile. She was getting it.

"I could choose to clean the house. It's a mess."

"That'd be great, but will you do it?"

"I'll do it. I will."

"What you just said and, I guess, the way you said it reminds me of something. Did you ever see the movie, *My Fair Lady?*"

"I did, the play and the movie. I was married. I had money then."

"Remember when Eliza started to speak correctly? Higgins and Pickering danced and sang. Do you know some of the words to that song?"

She gave me a look that said she didn't remember.

"They sang, 'She's got it, by Jove I think she's got it.' Or something like that. Teresa I think you've got it. So tell me, what do you know about everything you do? What do we all do before we do anything?"

She smiled and after a moment of thought she kind of sang,

"Choose it, by Jove I think we choose it."

"Will you call me after you clean the house. In fact, anytime you choose to do anything all week, call me and leave a message on my machine. Leave your number, and I'll find the time to call you back. Can you come next week at the same time?"

Teresa came quickly to the understanding that she is choosing all she does. But even that doesn't mean she's ready to act on this knowledge. In therapy, you can't predict how long it will take to get a client to this point. If I stick doggedly to the way I am dealing with Teresa, I would say no more than three sessions.

After this session, I waited a few days and then I talked at length to Janet. I told her what I did with Teresa and that she had called me twice to tell me she had chosen to do something constructive. She still didn't sound happy, but there was less evidence of the depression she had come in with. I told Janet what Teresa had said, "Too old for love, too young to die" and asked her,

"Have you read, *The Divine Secrets of the Ya-Ya Sisterhood*?

"I have; I loved it."

"I wonder if you'd be willing to start a Ya-Ya Sisterhood with some of our clients. They're alone too much. They're ashamed of being on welfare, of how little they're doing with their lives. I've heard that the Ya-Ya idea is taking hold in a few places. Why not with Teresa and some of our other clients? They're still stuck in the idea that they need a man for love. We need love. But we need it from any source we can get it. Why not get it from each other. And focus the group on doing things. The Ya-Yas did things; they didn't just sit around and feel sorry for themselves. I'll see Teresa next week and talk to her about it. You could lead a group here. I'll help you. I'd like to meet with them once in a while, too."

"Bill, I've been thinking about something like that. Right now there's a lot of pressure on us to get them back to work. I think this Ya-Ya idea has a lot going for it. I'll look over my caseload. I think if we can find a compatible group, it would work."

The next week Teresa was on time and looked better. She started right in by saying,

"You're right about one thing. I choose what I do. And I guess everything I don't do, too. And I've done some things, when I called you, I wasn't kidding. But it's so hard. Why is it so hard?"

"There're so few questions you can ask me that I can give a short, accurate answer to, but that's one I can. They're hard because you're all alone. Right now, you're what I call disconnected. You don't have anyone whom you know cares about you except your kids. You need other people."

"I need a man. But look at me, what man would be interested in me?"

"I'm not saying that you don't need a man. But do you

want to pin all your hopes on a man, or would you like to try something else?

"What else could I do?"

"Teresa, I have a book here. It's my book, but I've read it. You can keep it. It's the Ya-Ya book, have you heard of it?"

"No, I've never heard of it. What's it about?"

"It's about a group of wealthy women; they all have husbands and families."

She interrupted, "What in the world do these women have to do with me?"

"Be patient, give me a chance. I think they have a lot to do with you."

"Yeah, how?"

"They were lonely, they had problems. When you were still married and had money, didn't you have problems?"

"I thought I did. I was really out of it. Compared to now, I didn't have a worry in the world."

"Well it's *now* we have to deal with, and I'd like you to read this book. Then, if you're interested, Janet and I would like your help to start a Ya-Ya group. All women, close like sisters, always there for each other. You don't have to have money to care for another human being. Women know how to treat each other; you can see it in the book. And I want to make it perfectly clear that I'm not talking about sexual relationships. For thousands of years, women have supported women. It may even be why the human species has survived. I say, take advantage of your genetic good fortune. Care for each other."

12

George and Ellen

"He's suicidal? He wants to kill himself? What's wrong? For God's sake, tell me what's wrong?"

George stayed in Portland for almost two weeks. He called to tell me he was learning a lot about how other men coped with this problem, and he was anxious to see me as soon as he came home. When he came in, the change was remarkable. There was no sign of depressing; it seemed as if a load had been taken off his mind. He started right in. I barely had time to say hello.

"I met four women in the Portland area who used to be men. Their stories were almost identical to mine—even the thoughts about suicide."

"What was different?"

"Their wives. Their wives knew about their problem before the men had surgery. Their wives had even gone as far as going out with them and acting as if they were girlfriends when the men were cross-dressed as women. Their wives accepted that the operation was all that would satisfy them. They're on good terms with them and their children. In two instances in which there were children, the husbands and fathers became sisters to their wives and aunts to the children."

"How did you get in touch with these people?"

"Through the doctor; he seemed to have a great deal of understanding of my problem. I liked him. He also put me through a bunch of psychology tests, and I came up a woman in all of them. I'm ready to have the surgery, but I still haven't told my wife. I really don't know how to do it. The people I talked with couldn't believe I hadn't told my wife."

"Did they have any suggestions on how to do it?"

"No, but they all said I needed to do it. In fact, this surgeon won't operate on a married man without his wife's consent. I've got to tell her. But I know it's not going to be easy for her; I can't predict what she'll do."

"But you've made up your mind. You're going to have the operation?"

"Yes. . . . I have. I want what these men had. I want to look in the mirror and see a woman. I want a man just like a woman wants a man. But I like that doctor, so I've got to have my wife's permission. That's my problem. I need your help."

This was a ticklish situation. I wanted to help him, but I didn't know if I could. This was not therapy; therapy helps people. This would be hurting an innocent person. As far as she knew, nothing was wrong. I didn't even know if this was ethical. I said,

"George, this is new to me. It doesn't feel right. Those men told their wives; they didn't ask anyone else to do it. My feeling is that you should tell your wife. By the way, tell me her name. I don't want to have to keep calling her your wife."

"Her name is Ellen."

"I can help you to tell her; I'd be more than willing to do that. Just be here. I'm uncomfortable with the idea of being the first one to tell her. It doesn't seem right to me."

"I just can't tell her. I can't. You don't know her. I don't know what she might do. . . . I came to you for help. This is the help I need. Who else but you should I ask?"

He had a good point there. After he told me his problem, I could have said, "I can't help you." But I didn't want to. I was too curious. I'm still curious, but I'm also frightened. Since I just sat there, he continued.

"I don't want anyone else to tell her; I want you."

"Would you give me a letter absolving me of all responsibility if I tell her and she does something drastic?"

He nodded, and I continued, "How will you go about telling her she has to see me? How do you propose getting her here?"

"I'll tell her the truth. I'll tell her I have a serious problem that I've gone to you to talk about. And now you want to see her because the problem involves her."

"I'm sure she'll ask you what the problem is."

"I'll tell her, 'I'll talk to you about it after you see the doctor.'"

We talked a while longer, but there was really nothing to add to what he had to say. She'd come in. I was sure of that. And I'd tell her. I was sure of that, too. But how? I'd never done anything like this before. George kept assuring me I'd be fine, I guess trying to give me a little therapy.

He said, "It's not like I'm dying. I'm going to be fine. I'll still love her. But as a sister. That's what those men told me; that's the best way to look at it."

Ellen came to see me a few days after I talked with George. She was exquisitely dressed and beautifully made up. She was a very attractive woman who looked at least ten years younger than she must be. She had a kind, loving face. But she also looked worried but still confident as if she wasn't so worried she couldn't handle what the problem was. It was obvious to me that she didn't have the faintest idea what I was going to tell her. She sat down and just looked at me. She wasn't a woman to play her cards until she knew what the stakes were.

I asked, "What did George tell you when he told you he wanted you to see me?

"He said he'd seen you and he had a problem. I asked him what the problem was, and he said, 'I'll be glad to talk to you about it as soon as you see him.' So here I am. I guess I don't have to tell you that I don't like what's going on. If he has a problem, why can't he tell me?"

"Ellen, can I call you Ellen?"

She nodded.

"Ellen, I'd like to show you something; it's here in my desk. I just want you to take a look."

I opened my desk drawer, and she came and took a look.

"My God, I didn't know a psychiatrist needed a gun. Are you afraid of my husband? Why are you showing me that gun?"

"Does George keep a gun at home?"

"Not that I know of. But that's your gun, isn't it?"

Ellen was a smart woman. Even as she said, "It's your gun," I could see she doubted it. She was beginning to suspect something. After a pause, in which I gestured with my head to tell her it wasn't my gun, she said, "If it's his gun, what's it doing in your drawer?"

I nodded and said, "The first time I saw him a few weeks ago, I made him give it to me. I told him unless he did, I wouldn't see him."

"But why, why did he have a gun? Why did he show it to you?"

"He showed it to me and told me that unless I could help him, he was going to kill himself. I told him I'd help but not as long as he had the gun. He agreed to give it to me. It's not the first time this has happened."

"But he could just go out and get another one."

"He could, but if he really wants help, he won't do that. I just don't want it in his possession if he suddenly gets real down."

There was a long pause. I saw some tears form in her eyes. She quickly daubed her eyes, trying to avoid smearing her mascara. Then in a soft shriek, that's the best I can describe it, she said, "He's suicidal. He wants to kill himself. What's wrong? For God's sake, tell me what's wrong?"

"Did he seem upset when he told you to see me?"

"No, no, just the opposite. In fact, he just took a business trip to Portland. He stayed away for two weeks. He called me every night and seemed fine. But when he came back, he seemed happier than he's been in years. Tell me, please, what's wrong?"

I had to tell her, I said, "George isn't suicidal anymore. He's alive, and he plans to stay alive. But he has a problem. I don't think you could figure out what his problem is in a million years. I was totally surprised myself. When he came to see me, he'd about made up his mind to end his life. He told me he had played Russian roulette with this revolver twice. When the gun didn't go off, he took it as an omen and came to see me. When he told me what was wrong, the first thing I asked him was, 'Does Ellen know about this?' He assured me that you didn't. And he told me he was afraid to tell you. He begged me to see you and tell you. He was right when he told you he'd be glad to talk about it after you see me."

I paused as she continued to look at me with a mixture of puzzlement and horror.

"There's no easy way to say this. . . . He believes he's really a woman and he wants to have the operation. I'm sure you've heard about this sort of thing."

It was as if I'd hit her with a sledgehammer. George's words came back to me, "When she finds out about this, she'll decompensate." She was falling apart in front of my eyes. I didn't have any idea what to do or say. I just kept looking at her, sending the message that what I said was true.

She said, "I have to go to the rest room."

I handed her the key and just sat and waited. After about fifteen minutes, she came back. It was obvious that she had been crying, and she wasn't the kind of woman who cries in front of strangers. She'd gone to the rest room to try to put herself together. How she looked was very important to her.

I said, "I talked to George. I tried to get him to tell you. I didn't want to do this. But he said, 'If you really want to help me, you'll do this for me.'"

"How long has he known about this?"

"Since he was young, before he was a teenager. He should have told you before he got married, but he wasn't sure. He thought that marriage might change him. It didn't. Nothing can change him. He's planning to get the operation. He's found a surgeon in Portland who does this operation. He likes him. That's why he was so happy."

"But he's always been so loving. Was it all a sham?"

"Ellen, he does love you; he loves you very much. If he didn't love you, I'd have refused to tell you. But he doesn't love you as a man; that part is a sham. He loves you as a woman would love you."

She raised her eyebrows. "No, no, not as a lesbian; it's not that at all. It's more like a sister, a really close sister. But think, now that you know this, isn't there anything that he does or did that puzzled you, that maybe makes sense now?"

"Do you mean about sex?"

"I guess so. I didn't ask him about sex with you. I didn't because he was so upset. It wasn't really necessary for me to have that information."

I didn't ask her about sex either. I just looked at her as if she might want to tell me what she'd noticed.

"We've never had much sex. It's probably been years since we had intercourse. He told me he doesn't know why, but he just doesn't like sex. I've talked to a few women I know, and they told me some men quit sex. I didn't mind it because he's loving. He likes to be close to me; we still sleep together and embrace. I knew something was wrong, but what was I to do? I have a good life, he's a good companion, we have plenty of money. We talk about everything. . . . Well, everything but one thing."

"Has he shown any interest in your clothes? Or in women's clothes in general?"

"A lot of interest. One of the favorite things he likes to do is go shopping with me. He bought me this suit; actually, he bought me everything I have on. The blouse, the jewelry. Once in a while, he even buys me some undergarments. But we don't shop for that together. I have a fabulous wardrobe. He likes to buy clothes for all his employees at Christmas. But not only the women, the men, too. In fact, last year when we were shopping for Christmas presents together, he said, 'How about if I pick out the women's clothes and you pick out the men's?' That's what you're driving at, isn't it?"

I nodded; she was a fast learner. She seemed less upset as we talked about it. But then, in a kind of tongue-in-cheek manner, she said something that surprised me.

"I'm thinking I ought to buy a gun. Or maybe you should give me his. Someone in the family ought to use it."

I was pleased. She was trying to deal with the problem. She lightened up the conversation. That was a good sign. I took it as an opportunity to tell her what George told me the first time he saw me. I had no reason to keep anything back; he didn't ask me to. I disregarded her comments about the gun.

I said, "As happy as he seems, he needs something from you. The surgeon won't operate on a married man unless his wife gives her permission. He wants your permission. He told me he even wants you there when he's operated on. It's a lot to ask."

"It is a lot to ask. I'm going to have to think about that. I'm going to have to do a lot of thinking about this whole thing. But you tell me what you think. Is this what he really wants? I don't know much about it. If it doesn't work, I'd be real worried he'd kill himself then."

"I don't think either of us knows that much about this thing. I'm not claiming I'm any kind of expert. But I think he wants it so much he's more than willing to take that chance. I don't think you realize the extent of his problem. George doesn't want to live anymore. George is willing to die on that operating table.

"What do you mean?"

"I mean, he's going to die and be reborn as a forty-nine-year-old woman. He's going to feel just like a woman feels. He's going to feel like you feel, like almost all women feel."

"But how can that be? That operation can't really make him into a woman."

"It's what I'm trying to explain. He doesn't need the operation to feel like a woman. He already feels that way. He's felt that way since he was ten years old. He needs the operation to get his mind straight. He wants to see a woman when he looks in the mirror. He'd rather die than keep pretending."

Another long pause. She just looked at me. Then she said,

"Okay, he's all set. I'll help him get through the operation. Then what do I do?"

"Accept him as your sister. As your son's aunt. He doesn't want to get out of your life."

Another long pause, then she said, "I understand what you're talking about. But the way I feel right now, I don't want to do it. I can no more see myself in that role than he can see himself as he is now."

I agreed to tell her and I have. I feel no urge to try to persuade her to do anything. She doesn't seem suicidal or homicidal. She married a man. That man is going to be gone. I have no business trying to influence her about the way she will deal with what George is going to become. That's up to her.

"Ellen, what you do when he has that operation is up to you. All I agreed to do was to tell you. Whatever else happens is between you and George."

"Did he talk to you about his business, the travel agency? It's a big business. I worked with him at the start, but I haven't worked there for years."

"Talk to him; ask him all these questions. He wants to answer them. He told me you'll always be well provided for. He didn't say anything about giving up the business."

"How about you? You're involved; can I come and talk to you?"

"Absolutely, but I don't want you to think that you have to come and talk to me. As far as I'm concerned, there's nothing wrong with you. You had no way of knowing what he was when you married him. You had no way of knowing what he was until I just told you. I'm involved with George. If you feel you need some help, you may want to talk to another therapist—that might be a better idea."

There wasn't much more I could do in this interview, but Ellen was in no hurry to leave. She just sat there and reminisced about all the things that now made sense to her that seemed puzzling before.

She said, "He always tries to hire women. And he treats them all so well. He told me over and over, 'Women work hard, much harder than men, if you treat them well.' I was always surprised at how well he treated them. I'd never realized it, but I guess he thought like a woman. That was his secret. Well, doctor, I guess that's that."

I nodded and she left.

It didn't take long for George to call. He came in early the next day. I asked, "How is Ellen taking it?"

"That's what I came to talk to you about. By the way, I really appreciate you telling her. It was really a big favor."

"How was she when she got home?"

"Surprisingly calm. No hysterics. But she wanted to talk. We talked until the wee hours of the morning. She told me to tell you she wasn't going to come in any more. She said, 'There's nothing wrong with me. I don't need a therapist. I have no reason to see the doctor.'"

"What did you talk about?"

"The whole thing. She was trying to figure out if I was serious. It took her some time, but she said she was satisfied that this is what I want to do. Rather than decompensate, she seemed amazingly together. She'll sign the consent, but she wants a divorce right away. She wants a good financial settlement, and she's going to get her own lawyer. We've got money, and she says she doesn't want to have to worry about money anymore. She wants me to buy her a luxury condo and pay for it, no mortgage. And do it quickly."

"Is any of this a problem for you?"

"It's not the way I want it. You see, she doesn't want to see me again until at least a year after the operation. She said, 'If you need help, see Dr. Glasser.'"

"She won't go through it with you like you wanted?"

"That's it, exactly. It's up to me. If I have any kind of a happy life after I've had the surgery, she may agree to see me. But she won't guarantee it. Doctor, the way she was, was as if I was already dead. It was spooky."

"Can you accept that, that to her you're already dead . . . can you blame her? Ellen has no idea what Georgia will be like. I admire her. I think she's handling this very well. Better than I expected."

"But I talked to the other men who had the operation, their wives stuck by them. They're good friends now. I thought it would be that way with Ellen."

"Maybe you're better off than they are. She wants to start a new life. She married George, not Georgia. Don't you want a new life, too?"

"I do, but . . ."

"So get one. If you need help, see me. I'll be glad to see you, but if I were you, I'd go along exactly with what she asked. If you ever want to see her again, let her be. She's angry, George. And I think that's good. The anger is helping her. Stay out of her way unless she calls you. Wait for her to make the move. By the way, did you talk about your son?"

"We did for a long time."

"Did you decide anything?"

"She said I'd have to break the news to him and that we should see him separately for the foreseeable future. She laughed when I told her I wanted to be his aunt."

"Okay, so what can I do for you?"

"You can see me through this thing. I'll need somebody to talk to."

"I'd like to do that. I'd like to see you once a week, so we can really get to know each other.

And that's what happened. Before George left for the surgery, he did talk to his son, and he was okay with it. He was competent, on his own, and had no serious relationships—no one he had to tell immediately. I saw George up until the operation, and I expected he'd come back soon after, but he didn't. He stayed in Portland for almost a year. When he finally came back and came to see me, I had to admit to myself that I was startled. I'd expected a change, but I was not prepared for the tall, attractive woman he'd become. I guess it shouldn't have surprised me, but it did. He'd also gotten what he really wanted: He'd fallen in love with a man in Portland and said the man was in love with him. I asked him, "Does he know you used to be a man?"

"I've told him everything. He says he loves me, that he's never known me except as a woman, so what I used to be doesn't make any difference. He's going to come down here to live with me as soon as he can get a job. It'll be no problem for him; he's already had a few good offers."

"Now that you're back, have you made any effort to see Ellen?"

"I called her, but she didn't want to talk and she won't see me. She has a new love in her life, and she doesn't want him to know anything about me. I can respect that."

All this happened several years ago, but everything seems fine. As I thought the whole thing over, I believe that the best thing I did for him was to keep him from committing suicide and that I did see his wife. He didn't hold it against me that I didn't try to persuade her to remain friends with him.

I saw Georgia only once when she came back. After she had the operation, she didn't need any more help from me. She told me that the women who ran the business were doing a great job and that they had no trouble accepting her as a woman. She doesn't want to work much longer, and she's making arrangements for them to buy the business. For a while, she'll work a day or two a week to help, and they appreciate it. The surgery didn't affect her business skills.

13

JUDITH

We opened the door, and there she was: naked in bed with a boy about her age, busily engaged in sex.

Judith was one of the most interesting young women I've ever seen in therapy. Her parents were concerned about her and came in to see me. They were both highly educated, he a geneticist, she a public accountant. They appeared to be in their late fifties; otherwise there was nothing remarkable about either their looks or their mannerisms. I did consider them a little old to be parents of a sixteen year old, but I didn't say anything. It didn't seem pertinent to ask.

Whenever parents come to see me about a teenager, I expect a rebellious child, which Judith was, but in a far different way than any teenager I'd seen before or since. I won't go into the whole conversation; there was a lot of getting-acquainted small talk, but the following is the important part of what we talked about.

Dad: We don't want you to get the wrong impression. I mean she's not crazy or using drugs or alcohol, and she's a top student in a good high school. And she likes school. She's never been in any trouble; up to now she's never given either of us a hard time about anything. She spends the money we give her on books and classical CDs. She's aware we're coming to see you, and she said, 'That's fine with me.' She says the problem's ours anyway; she's believes she's okay the way she is.

Mom: Doctor, I don't think she's fine at all. She needs help; that's why we're here.

She turned to me and said,

Mom: There's no sense beating around the bush. She's a late-life child. I was forty-three when she was born. We also have two boys, both in their early thirties, both married with children. She gets along fine with her brothers; one lives here in town and she's especially close to his wife. We travel a lot, but since she's been twelve she prefers to stay by herself. She's totally self-sufficient, and the house is always immaculate when we come back. We've offered to get a college student in to stay with her, but she says, No. If she needs anything she can call on her brother or his wife. She can drive now, and we leave her a car. She's a very careful driver; we don't worry about her at all.

She then looked at her husband, and I looked at them as if to say, *What's wrong? She sounds perfect.* Then she said,

Mom: Go ahead, you tell him.

Dad: About a week ago, we came home from a trip on a Friday afternoon around five. Now that she drives, she offered to pick us up, but we got an earlier plane, much earlier; we were supposed to be back at ten. We decided not to call her, just to come home. We didn't want her to have to change any plans.

Mom: As soon as we walked in the door, we heard something going on in her room. It's the only bedroom on the ground floor, and she's used it since she was small. She liked it because it was separate from her brothers and it has it's own bathroom. Anyway . . . we opened the door, and there she was: naked in bed with a boy about her age, busily engaged in sex. She didn't see us or hear us, and for about a minute we both just stood there. I mean this was totally unexpected. Finally, I said, "Judy, what are you doing?" and she said, cool as a cucumber, as if nothing at all had happened, "Mother, I keep telling you my name is Judith; please don't call me Judy." I mean it was surreal.

Dad: I don't want to sound like a prude, but in that situation you'd expect that she'd have been contrite and worried about what we'd think.

Mom: But she wasn't; she wasn't at all. She glared at us. She was upset because she'd been interrupted.

Dad: She was angry. She asked us what we were doing home. She said that it was her room, and she had a right to do what she wanted in it.

Mom: The boy was scared to death, and Judy told us to get out. That they'd get dressed, and she'd drive him home. She'd talk to us later if we wanted to talk about it.

Dad: And that's what happened. We didn't have any idea of what else to do. We left them, and in about fifteen minutes she came out and introduced the young man. He was about her age, and she told us he was a classmate. He was still uncomfortable, but he offered his hand and we shook it. She drove him home, and we were beside ourselves. I mean the way she talked is as if this has been going on for a long time and there was nothing for us to worry about.

Mom: Something's wrong; this isn't normal behavior. When she came home, she said that her having sex was none of our business. She'd been having it since she was thirteen, and she enjoyed it. She had no intention of stopping, and she was really glad that we knew. She wouldn't have to sneak around anymore. She wasn't backing down at all.

Dad: We don't want to sound as if she is Miss Goody Two-shoes, but mostly she's quiet—studying, reading, and listening to classical music. But whenever she is frustrated, she has no problem opening her mouth. Not so much to us, but she's been letting her teachers know what is on her mind since the second grade. She's criticized their ability to teach and the stupid assignments they've given her. But her work has always been of such high quality that there hasn't been much they could do. There were teachers who liked her and whom she liked, so after a blowup, she'd ask for a transfer, and mostly she'd get it. It hasn't happened that much, but when it has, it has taken a while to calm things down. The school didn't blame us; we were willing to do what we could, but mostly we didn't do anything. Once in a while, not so much lately, she'd get into an intellectual discussion with us; we had to be on our toes when we argued with her.

Mom: But this is different. It's not right; there's something really wrong. We want you to see her.

Doc: Have you approached her about seeing me? I'm leery about seeing her if she doesn't know who I am.

Dad: Of course she knows. My God, we don't do anything unexpected with her.

Mom: When we discussed it, she said if you had any brains at all, you'd support what she was doing. She made it clear that the problem is ours, not hers.

Dad: She'll be fine with you. We're not asking for any guarantees. Just talk to her; see if she needs some help.

We talked a little more, but that was the basic information. The good part was that Judith wanted to see me; the bad part was that I didn't think I could do much with her. I have no magic words to persuade a highly sexed sixteen year old to give up sex. But her folks hadn't gone off the deep end with a lot of threats they couldn't back up; that was the good news.

Judith came in a few days later, and I was surprised that she was so conservatively dressed; wore no makeup; and had long, clean, dark brown hair. She was a young-looking sixteen year old. I'd expected a teenager who might be making an effort to be sexy and mature, but she was neither. She was pretty in an intellectual sort of way, but looking at her would never give anyone the impression that she was involved with sex or even had a smart mouth. She also was calm, friendly, and seemed very much at ease.

I started by saying, "Your folks told me the story—their coming home early, the argument that followed. They want me to see you because they think you may want to talk to someone. I guess the first question I ought to ask is, Do you think you need therapy?"

"I don't know if I need it, but I'm very willing to talk with you. If you think I need it, tell me. I'm not like my folks; I don't close my mind to anything. Besides, if you're intelligent and can carry on a conversation, I'll enjoy it. I love to talk to people worth talking to, and believe me, they're hard to find. And don't worry about the money; they've plenty of money. What would you like to talk about?"

As you can see, there would be no trouble talking with her.

But what I like is her friendliness. I just have to avoid saying anything stupid. And not to say or do anything that smacks of external control. I'm sure she sees herself as the equal of or superior to almost anyone she meets. This is sure to be interesting.

"Well, I guess the first thing to ask you about is sex. That's what your folks are worried about, so why don't we start with that? I don't really have any questions; tell me anything you think I ought to know."

"I like that. I think it would be fun to talk to an adult about sex; I've done that a little bit with my brother's wife. I had to because I needed birth control pills. I have no intention of getting pregnant. I had to do a lot of talking because I was only thirteen. She was a little reluctant, but I told her that if she wanted to tell my folks, it was okay with me. And if she didn't want me to get pregnant, she'd get the pills for me. She's cool. Once in a while she asks, 'Is everything okay?' I always tell her everything's fine, and she's been getting me the pills. After a while she got nervous and told her doctor that she was giving some of the pills he prescribed to me. Her doctor asked me to come in, and I did. I got a checkup, and I'm fine. I have no trouble with the pills. After they discovered me, my mother asked me about birth control. I told my folks about my sister-in-law getting the pills for me. If it wasn't for her, I might have had to use condoms or withdrawal to avoid getting pregnant. Would you want to have that kind of sex?"

I was fascinated with her way of dealing with life. I didn't say anything. I just encouraged her to go on.

"When I told my parents about the pills, they were relieved, happy she'd helped me out. They love her; they weren't angry with her for not telling them what I was doing. Like I told them, I'm glad it's out in the open now; I hate to sneak around."

I just looked at her. She was having a good time talking. I didn't have to say anything. She continued.

"I guess it must be obvious to you that I like sex. I liked it right from the first time I did it, and I've almost always enjoyed it. I believe that this is the best time in your life to make love. Why in the world wait for something that feels this good? If nature didn't want me to have sex at my age, it wouldn't feel so good. It's not like I'm doing anything wrong. What's wrong with careful, safe sex?"

"Do you stick with one guy, or do you have more than one guy going at a time?"

"No, no. Just one guy at a time. I'm looking for a lot more than sex."

"For love?

"For love? No, I don't think so. I agree with people who say that at my age, you're too young for love. Love, marriage, and children, that's serious business. I know I'm not ready for that. Sex is fun. I don't have to pretend I'm in love to enjoy it. Truthfully, Doctor. I don't even know how love feels."

"But you said you're looking for a lot more than sex."

"I am. I'm very particular about the guys I go to bed with. The one I'm with now is the best so far."

"What do you mean, *particular*?"

"Wouldn't you be particular about who you went to bed with? Why would I be any different from you?"

I've got to be careful. This young woman is razor sharp. She took that question as a put-down. She doesn't have much respect for adults, and that was a stupid question.

She went on, "I guess my mom told you I started at thirteen. Actually, I was thirteen and a half and quite mature. I'm not much bigger now than I was then. But I don't wear clothes that show my figure; my figure is my own business. Dressing sexy is stupid. Sex is for bed; it's not for the street. But after that first time when I found out it was so good, I did a lot of thinking. I guess you've figured out I'm not impulsive. I made up my mind that I wanted to keep having sex. But not again with that first guy. He was scared to death. I didn't like that. What's to be scared of? We didn't do it in the street. Anyway I spent a lot of time figuring out who I wanted to go to bed with."

As she told me this story, I thought to myself, *What could I do with her?* I'm certainly not going to try to get her to stop having sex. Any move in that external-control direction would turn her off completely. But I don't feel as if I have to do anything but listen. That's all her folks asked me to do. And really at this point, that's all I want to do. I'll try to get to know her and see what happens. I just kept listening, and she continued.

"This is what I've figured out, and it's been working fine for almost three years. It has to be the right guy. Not the kind of guys the girls at school think are sexy, the idiots who play football and basketball. Do you know that some of those guys beat up the girls they go with? They want to dominate them, and the idiot girls think it's love. I don't know much about love, but I know that being dominated has nothing to do with it. Believe me, no one's ever going to dominate me."

"What kind of guy is right for you?"

"First of all, he has to be smart. Not as smart as me—that'd be too high a standard—but still plenty smart. I want a guy who reads and thinks. And enjoys classical music. I want someone who likes to talk and hasn't watched so much TV he's forgotten how. I want a guy who's gentle, who wants to learn what pleases me, who cares how I feel. I want a guy who could be my best friend if we weren't having sex. The guys I've had and then stopped with are still my friends. I have no difficulty finding them. . . . I look around in school, I watch the guys in class. As you may have guessed, most of them are scared of me at first because I speak out in class a lot. But when one of them joins in and says something sensible, that's a guy who interests me. So I make it my business to talk with him. It took me a while to figure out how to do that because none of these guys have ever had sex. That a girl with my brains would approach them about sex is beyond their comprehension. But as soon as they find out I'm really interested, bingo. But I go slow; I ask them to come to my house. Mostly there's no one home. Then we go into my bedroom and turn on some good music. We talk about music, about a book we've read. Most of these guys read. One thing: At their age, you don't have to do anything to get them excited. Most of them can do it at least twice; a few, three times. I tell them no masturbating in between. But I don't really care if they do."

"I can see how you get started, but you've had a few guys. Do you get tired of them? How do you get rid of a boy if you want another one?"

"After a while, I want someone new. But it's not because I'm tired of them. I just want a new experience and, like I said, I don't want more than one at a time. I explain to them that what we have is good, but I want to have this experience with someone new. I tell them that what we're doing is just the opposite of marriage. Once you get married, the rule is no one new. I respect that rule. But I think that having a lot of good teenage experiences is a great way to prepare for that eventuality. I plan to keep doing this until I leave for college. I'm not sure what I'll do then. But I've got plenty of time for that.

"Aren't you worried about a guy falling in love with you? Maybe getting real upset about you moving on?"

"You mean like threatening to kill himself?

"Or kill you?"

"It's happened. I don't mean killing himself, but a couple did say they loved me and couldn't live without me. But so far I've stuck to my guns. I remind them that I'd told them before we started that I'll end it. But we could still be friends, and it's worked out that way. I've told them this wasn't love and it wasn't for keeps. And it's been great. For all I know, this may be the best sex of my life."

"But don't you care about your reputation? There must be some talk."

"There is a little, and I like it. One of the guys I've been with knew a little about me; it helped. But the few guys who've found out are creeps. What would I care what they say? If I was five girls, I'd never run out of the kind of guy I like. The macho guys don't really know anything about me. When I talk in class, they think they're hearing Sanskrit."

"I've got to be truthful. I've never met anyone of any age, much less your age, who's done this much thinking about sex. I just worry it's too easy. It may seem to be only sex, but you're playing with love and that's dangerous. A couple of guys claim they have fallen for you. This could be serious."

"Look, I'm not a machine. I have fallen a little for almost all of them. But that's what makes it so good. But I guess you don't realize how carefully I pick these guys. These are intelligent guys, not the jealous, macho jocks who pride themselves on their conquests. I've been good to them, and they've been very good to me. So far no trouble. And I'm not needy. I like the guys, but I don't need them. Right now, I can't see myself ever needing a man like those airhead chicks who hang around the jocks. But look, you're right. I am playing with love, and I may get hurt. But if I fall in love, I'll have to deal with it. But don't you see, that's why I wanted to see you. If I have any problem, I won't be alone, you'll help me. But no matter what happens, I'd like to have someone to talk with. I'm glad my folks caught us."

"Look, Judith. I'd like to see you and talk with you. I think you're fascinating, but I've got to tell your folks this whole story. They've got to know that I'll help you with your whole life, but I'm not going to try to get you to stop doing what you're doing. If knowing all you've told me, they're still willing for me to see you, I'd like to very much. Can I tell them what you've told me?"

"It's fine with me. I'd be happy to tell them all this myself, but it'll be less traumatic if you do it. Emphasize that I'm not trying to hide anything from them. But I would appreciate it if they would allow me to see you."

We talked a little while longer about all her interests. She was an omnivorous reader and, as you have already seen, a great conversationalist. My dilemma was that besides telling her parents the truth, all I was going to do is what they asked: see her, talk with her. If she messes up her life, at least she'll have me to talk with. But I don't think she's going to mess up her life.

I also have the same problem her folks have. The way she's

behaving is literally flouting the morality of the whole world. Do I have some duty to work on this with her? Well, let's see what happens. I've got to talk to her folks.

I got in touch with the parents and asked them to come in. Over the phone, I told them I'd had a real good talk with Judith and she wanted to keep seeing me. But before I'd agree to continue to see her, we'd have to talk in the office. In a few days they both came in. I started by saying, "I'm sure you know that you have a very interesting daughter."

Mom: What did she tell you?

I repeated the whole story. Then I asked them what they wanted to do. Dad spoke up next.

Dad: We don't know what to do. But what she's doing isn't right. Can't you stop her?

Doc: There's not a thing I can do except talk with her and establish a relationship. She says she needs someone to talk with. She can't talk to either of you; she says it would end up in a fight. I believe her; you don't seem in the mood to listen.

Mom: Can't we send her somewhere, somewhere where they'll keep her from doing what she's doing?

Doc: It's possible. You could find a psychiatrist who'd pin some kind of sexual disorder diagnosis on her and be willing to hold her in a hospital. She's still a minor; you could sign her in. But I'll tell you. If you do that, my guess is you'll lose her. This girl is tough; she'll never forgive you. And I don't think they'd keep her very long unless they drugged her into insensibility. Would you want to risk that? I'll tell you she's as smart as any psychiatrist she'll see. She'll figure out a way to get out. I wouldn't envy anyone who tried to control her. All you can do is leave her alone. I mean, love her and certainly talk to her but not about this. The more she thinks you're at war with her, the more she'll fight. She has great potential. I don't think you want to lose her.

Mom: Are you willing to see her?

I nodded.

Doc: I'd like to see her once a week. It'll take time, but we'll get to know each other. If she messes up, I'll be there to help, but I don't think she will.

Dad: But what if she wants to bring a boy to our house?

Doc: Talk it over with her. Tell her never when you're home. You travel a lot; wouldn't you be better off knowing she's safe in your own home?

Mom: But isn't that illegal?

Doc: I'd talk to a lawyer about that. And if you do, take her with you. Don't do anything behind her back. But please don't get the police involved. . . . If that's what you're thinking about, I won't see her. Judith is a gifted person. She's not really a child; let's be careful not to lose her.

Her parents were desperately trying not to lose her. They were doing the best they could by getting her psychiatric help. I couldn't predict what she'd do if they got the police involved. But whatever it would be, it would be destructive to the whole family. I have to do my best to make a good relationship with her, and then I may be able to help her to see her parents' point of view.

So that's what happened. I saw Judith every week for the next year. We talked about everything. There seemed to be nothing she wasn't interested in. During that year, she finished with the boy who'd been in bed with her and had one more. She saw him up until she went to college back east. He stayed in California, so I guess it ended. I never saw her after her last visit, but she called me to say good-bye when she went off to college.

One question that kept running through my mind was this: Was I justified in seeing her for so long if nothing really changed? I broached that subject twice with her parents, and they begged me not to quit. I also talked to her about it, and with her usual candor she said, "If you want me to fake a nervous breakdown, I'll be glad to do it. I think it'd be fun."

But about three months after I first saw her, I did bring up something that turned out to be therapeutic.

I said, "I want to talk to you about something. It's very important to me, and I think it's important to you."

She looked at me as if to say go ahead.

"I'm worried about how you're treating your folks. I've called them and they seem satisfied, but I still wonder. Tell me, what's going on in your house?"

"Nothing, really nothing. I'm very good, but I go my way and they go theirs.

"That's what I mean. Are you satisfied to go your way and for them to go theirs?"

"They seem satisfied. It's hard to talk with them."

"Judith, nothing's hard for you. You know what I'm driving at."

"Look, whenever I see them, I see disapproval in their eyes."

"Wouldn't you want their approval?"

"How could I get it?"

"You figure out how to answer that question. You live there; I can't answer it."

"I don't have to tell them I'm going to stop what I'm doing?"

"Are they asking you to?"

"No, they haven't said a word. But it's better, with my latest guy; we mostly go to his house."

"It may be better, but it's still far from good. Your folks are scared of you. Do you want them to be scared?"

I took a chance when I told her this. Generally, it's not a good idea to tell any child of any age that her folks are intimidated by her. That gives the child a sense of power that can damage the relationship even further. But I didn't think it would work that way with Judith, and it didn't.

"I've got to talk to them, don't I? To be more friendly."

"Like you are with me. Tell them what we talk about; let them know you love them. You can do it. How could it hurt?"

"I'm being petty, aren't I?"

"I think so."

"You have any suggestions?"

"Tell them the truth. Tell them we talked about this. Tell them you want to start talking to them. Tell them to buy tickets to a play and ask them to buy one for your boyfriend, too. Afterward, talk about the play together. Right now, they're worried they'll lose you when you go away to college. They're good people. But they need to know you love them and you enjoy being with them. Figure it out. My ideas may not be as good as what you can come up with."

If we hadn't built a good relationship, I couldn't talk to her that way. She took her time, but in a couple of months they'd rebuilt what they'd lost and even gone further.

Her folks called me when she left for college and thanked me for all I'd done. I thanked them for making it possible for me to see her. About ten years later, when I was shopping, I ran into them. They were very happy to see me and proudly regaled me with all her accomplishments. They were on good terms with her. She was even engaged to be married.

14

ROGER

Alcohol gives Roger a temporary reprieve from external control and a temporary excuse to be more controlling.

Roger is an alcoholic, by far the most common addiction of the Western world. But no matter what drug addicts choose to use, drugs provide them with what they want above all else: easy and sure access to more pleasure than they believe they can get in any other way. Addicting drugs mimic or activate the pleasure-producing brain chemistry that has evolved to inform us that one or more of our basic needs is being satisfied.

In normal living, it takes some directed effort to satisfy a need. We are motivated to make this effort both by the unavoidable pain of not satisfying the need and the promise of pleasure if we do. If you are hungry or lonely, food or friendship rarely comes walking through the door. Big-time mountain climbers spend half their lives pursuing the joy of standing on the summit of Mount Everest, for them the ultimate power trip.

Since pain is the inevitable price we pay when we fail to satisfy our needs to the extent that we want to, we *must* attempt to do something to reduce it. For example, almost all the symptoms of the clients in this book, ranging from Jerry's obsessing to George's depressing, were their best efforts at the time to reduce the pain of their frustrated lives.

Painful or disturbing as these symptoms may be, choice

theory explains that they diminish the pain. But few of us are willing to settle for this small reduction. Almost everyone, including the people I counseled, want to replace the pain or painful symptom with pleasurable behaviors that they can continue to use. For example, George became a woman and Jerry got involved with Carol, but to do so they had to exert a lot of effort.

Addicting drugs are unique; they eliminate the need to expend much effort to gain huge amounts of pleasure. They are like gamblers who win the lottery by buying a dollar ticket. For that tiny effort, the gamblers get more money than they could make if they worked five hundred years. To an addict, the sure pleasure the drug will provide is well worth whatever effort is needed to get it. In Roger's case, the effort is minimal; alcohol is legal and available everywhere. But legal or illegal, the effort to get the drug is never much of a deterrent.

Even the obvious fact that their use of drugs can destroy their lives and the lives of people who depend on them does not deter addicts from pursuing this pleasure. That the drug can be harmful rarely crosses their minds and *never* does if they are successful in getting it. It is this sure pleasure, coupled with the total relief of pain, that takes over their minds. Even at the end of a long addiction, when most of the pleasure has been lost, what still remains embedded in their brains is the hope that *this time,* they will regain the pleasure they used to have. That hope will continue to motivate them until *somehow* they begin to give up on it. That *somehow* is the goal of all therapy with addicts.

To treat addicts, the treatment must persuade them to settle for the normal pleasures of life, pleasures that are longer lasting but much less intense than those a drug can provide. If it is successful, the treatment will reduce their *hope* for the pleasure of the drug enough so they can do without it. Most addicts tell me that this hope never completely leaves. But if they can start enjoying the normal pleasures of life—satisfying their needs sufficiently–that hope can be kept under control.

For this reason, it is important not to talk about their pleasurable drug experiences when treating addicts; this talk will raise that hope. But even talk about their miserable experiences should be curtailed. It too, is counterproductive because all the addicts will think about as they talk is how much better their lives would have been in that situation if they could have gotten more of the drugs with no hassle. Although the people I counseled, except Judith, were well aware of past discomfort, addicts pay little attention to past misery. They dismiss the pain and recall only the pleasure.

The only effective treatment, no matter what the method, is the same with addicts as with all other clients:

1. Focus on helping all clients learn new behaviors to recapture old relationships or gain new ones. Old or new, these relationships should be satisfying enough so the nonaddicts no longer need the symptoms and the addicts no longer need the drugs.
2. Therapists should not try to force or pressure any client, including an addict, to change.

But with an addict, both these treatment goals are much more difficult to achieve than with other clients. For example, the addict is being asked to give up the sure pleasure of the drug for the unpredictable pleasures of good relationships. And the therapist is continually *tempted* to try to convince the addict to give up the drug.

With almost all other clients, except addicted gamblers, the therapist doesn't have to ask them to give up the pain or symptom— that's what brought them into therapy. All the clients in this book except Judith wanted to get rid of their painful behaviors and work toward making this choice in therapy. Only Judith, like an addict, wanted to hang on to her pleasure. Addicts are difficult to treat because they are not interested in changing their behavior; they have found the pleasure they are seeking. They resist treatment. They see treatment as taking away their pleasure.

Another difficulty for an addict—other clients rarely have to contend with this problem—is that all the important people in the addict's life—family members, friends, employers, and even some professional counselors—try to convince the addict to give up the drug. When they do so, they are eliminating any chance the addict has to recapture the satisfying relationships he or she once had with these people. Although it wasn't hard to figure out that Jerry needed a good relationship with a woman, it never occurred to anyone who knew him to try to force him in this direction.

With an alcoholic, such as Roger, it's crystal clear to everyone around him that what's wrong is his drinking. But the clarity of Roger's problem is also a trap because it never occurs to anyone that trying to pressure Roger to stop drinking is counterproductive to what he really needs: a satisfying relationship. And since external control is the commonsense psychology of the whole world, everyone important to him is *threatening, punishing, criticizing, blaming, complaining, nagging,* and *enabling* to try to get him to stop.

Now that he has been drinking for close to twenty years and comes to see me, he's almost given up trying to connect and spends his time drinking and lying about how much he drank. He has little concern that he's doing anything wrong because he no longer cares very much how the people he needs feel. Besides, it's not as if what they are doing works; it makes things worse, not better, and no one knows that more than Roger. So as long as no one actually stops him from drinking, Roger pays only lip service to these efforts.

But then—I believe it to be his good fortune—Roger was picked up and charged with driving under the influence of alcohol (DUI), his second offense, and put in jail. For the first time, acting on advice from a court counselor and with the support of an Al-Anon group she attended, his wife did not bail him out. She visited him in jail and told him she was no longer going to enable his drinking. She said that she loved him and would stand by him, but he would have to work his way out of this scrape on his own. When Roger got to court, besides losing his license to drive, the judge gave him the choice of seeing me once a week plus attending four Alcoholics Anonymous (AA) meetings each week or going to jail.

What the judge did is an appropriate use of external control. He was not trying to establish a relationship with Roger; rather, he was making it possible for Roger to get better treatment than jail. The judge was also well aware of his legal responsibility to the community. Lives were in danger whenever Roger got behind the wheel of a car, so the judge wanted feedback on his progress. I was sure that Roger neither wanted to see me nor go to AA, that his main motivation for seeing me was to stay out of jail. But that did not deter me. All I demand of any client, voluntary or forced, is that he or she comes to see me. The rest is my responsibility.

Reality therapy does not supersede the law. The legal responsibility is the court's, and the court's psychology is always external control. My responsibility is to keep the court informed. For example, I will not try to protect Roger if he is picked up again for DUI or any other alcohol-related crime. I will inform the court if he stops seeing me, but I will let the court figure out how to confirm that he is attending AA meetings. I will also do my best to help Roger, but I will not extend myself by promising help as much as I do with nonaddicted clients. The first time he comes in, I will immediately make my position clear to him.

Furthermore, I will try to instruct all the people who are legally involved with him, such as his wife and employer, to stop enabling him, and I will try to teach his wife and other family members to replace external control psychology with choice theory. If Roger is to stop drinking, these are the people he has to reconnect with. As long as they use external control psychology, there is little chance for him to do so.

Although I am supportive of AA and the judge's decision

to make it a part of the treatment, I believe Roger has a much better chance of stopping drinking if he will continue both to see me and attend AA. He could attend AA meetings for the rest of his life, and he, I, and the court will mutually determine when he is ready to stop seeing me.

What I can try to provide is a satisfying, personal, choice-theory relationship, along with teaching him the choice theory he needs to know. All this will help him benefit from AA, since its philosophy is not incompatible with choice theory. Making connections is the heart and soul of AA. It's hard for anyone who attends to feel alone.

From the start, I know I have to come across to Roger differently from the way family members and friends, and perhaps even other counselors he may have seen in the past, have done. My plan is to try *never to use external control psychology,* for example, never even tell him he has to stop drinking. No matter what he does, I will never criticize, blame, complain, or nag. I have to model the kind of relationship he needs if he is to stop drinking. In as many variations as I can figure out, I will ask him one of the key reality-therapy questions: *Does drinking help you to get closer to the people you need?*

Roger's referral form contained the following information: age forty-two, married to his first wife, three teenage children, and a good job as a middle manager for a company that has been very patient with him. But the employer's patience is at an end. The next time he misses work, as he recently did for two weeks while he was in jail, it is almost certain that he will be fired.

Although his wife is willing to stick with him, his marriage is badly strained. Almost all his friends have given up on him; his present relationships were mostly with other drinkers. Unless he and I can quickly achieve a strong relationship, supplemented by the supportive relationships of AA, there is little chance for success.

When Roger came in, he already had the beginning looks of an alcoholic: clean but not neat, red eyes, and very nervous.

He kept adjusting his clothes and his position in the chair as if he couldn't get comfortable. I started with the following facts-of-life speech. It is vital that he understands both my position and that his situation is very serious. I also had this speech written out. I was going to ask him to sign two copies, one for him and one for me. As it turned out, he didn't resist.

"Roger, good to meet you. What we'll do here is talk. That's all. No Valium or any other medication. But before we start, I want to tell you what I do when I work with people with your problem. If you don't agree with what I'm going to tell you, then you can go back to the court and ask for another referral. Don't feel you're under any pressure to see me. First, I believe you're an alcoholic, and I will not argue that point. All that means to me is that you are having problems with drinking and need help to stop. You can't help yourself. I'm sure you've heard the argument that alcoholism is a disease caused by alcohol and, if you want to think you have it, that's fine with me. The disease may not be curable in the sense that you'll lose the desire to drink, but it is treatable by stopping drinking even though the desire will remain.

If you can stop drinking, you can lead a much more responsible life. When we talk, I may make suggestions, but I'm never going to tell you what to do. I am, however, an agent of the court, and I will have to inform the judge if you stop seeing me. Or if you tell me you are driving while continuing to drink. Besides you, the first person I want to talk with, always with you present, is your wife. If you want me to, I'll talk with anyone else, for example, your boss. I know that this seems like a lot to throw at you as soon as we meet. But my experience tells me that you don't think your drinking is a serious problem and that you really don't want to see me or go to AA. You're here because it's better than going to jail. But I'll tell you, Roger, and on this I'm sure you'll agree: Seeing me, is a thousand times better than going to jail. Do you have any questions?"

Roger just sat there and looked at me. It was as if he'd expected this lecture and it didn't really mean that much to him.

Finally, he said, "Look, Doc, you do what you have to do. . . . I don't want to go to jail. . . . And my wife does want to see you. She's going to pick me up after we're finished. If she can, she'll come early so if you want to see her you can."

This response is typical. He's already telling me "to do what I have to do" but don't count on him to help. The same for his wife, "She wants to see me." Not he wants her to see me so we can work out some of his problems with her help.

I wanted to get his opinion of AA, so I asked, "Do you understand you have to go to four AA meetings a week? That's a lot. AA will confirm to the court that you attended. Do you understand that?"

"Yeah, I talked to my probation officer about it. He gave me the name of a guy I have to call. I thought I'd see you first. I've been to a few meetings; they're okay. But I don't see how they help. A lot of guys go out drinking after the meeting. I went for a while a few years ago, and I did that a few times myself. But don't worry, I'll call the guy. I don't want to go to jail."

I think you can see my problem. To Roger, it's all external control: me, his wife. the probation officer, and the court. He hasn't a glimmer of the idea that he should do something to help himself. Right now I can hear his brain saying, *I could really use a drink*. I have to say something to try to get his attention that is totally different from what I've just said. That was all external control; from now on, I'll try to stick completely with choice theory with Roger.

"Roger, do you have the feeling, at home, at work, with your family and friends, even here with me, that everyone's always telling you what to do? That people are criticizing you, blaming you, complaining about you, nagging at you? You know what I mean."

He paused. I think that question got through a little. He said, "Doc, I've had that feeling my whole life. How did you know?"

"Because we all get that feeling once in a while. You can't find anyone who doesn't have that feeling to some extent, but my guess is that you have it a lot more than most people. Tell me, is there anyone in your life now who accepts you the way you are—drinking, DUI, the whole nine yards."

Now he was concentrating; this question interested him. He said, "Not now, nobody. Well, maybe some of the guys I drink with. Nobody else does. But before, when I was a kid, my grandma did, but she's been gone a long time. Since I started drinking, no one accepts me. Well, maybe my wife does. But when she didn't bail me out this time, I don't know about her anymore. To the rest of them, I'm a drunk. All the people at work know about my arrest; it was in the paper. They look at me funny-like since I've been back. Like I should be staggering around with a bottle in my hand or something like that."

"Tell me, are you that way, too? Do you tell people what to do? Like your wife, your kids, the people you manage at work?"

"Me, a drunk? Who would listen to me?"

"I don't mean when you're drinking, I mean when you're sober. You don't drink at work, do you?"

"No, never. I get the urge, but I've never had a drop. But you're right. When I'm sober, I'm a bear at times, kind of a know-it-all."

"How about missing work? How's your attendance?"

"That's what pisses me off. If she'd bailed me out, I wouldn't have missed a day. I'm in big trouble because I missed two weeks."

"Are you still able to do your job okay? Do the people who give you the looks listen to what you say?

"They'd better. The guys I boss know better than to goof off when I tell them what to do."

This is the real tragedy of external control: The people who are the most hurt by it, like Roger, use it the most. It becomes a vicious circle. The people he manages are now paying less attention to what he says: "Look funny at him," that's how he put it. This disrespect frustrates him, and he gets more controlling and it harms the relationships that are the requisite for effective managing. And it's even worse at home. His wife keeps trying to control him, and he resists in every way he can, including drinking. External control poisons every relationship in which it is used. Alcohol gives Roger a temporary reprieve from external control and a temporary excuse to be more controlling. And as long as he drinks, nothing will change. But if he could learn to stop drinking, there would be less need for his boss to try to control him at work and his wife to try to control him at home. And less need for him to try to control his wife and the people who work for him. I'll begin by teaching both Roger and, I hope, his wife, choice theory; home is where it's needed most right now. As long as he doesn't drink at work or lose days, he'll keep his job.

"Roger, let's talk about your wife. She knows you're seeing me today. You came here from work. You can't drive. How'd you get here?"

"My wife dropped me off this morning. A friend from work drove me here after work. I told him I had to see a doctor. She's going to swing by to pick me up. She should be here any minute."

"Would it be all right if I ask her to come in. I'd like us all to talk together. Would that be okay with you?"

There's no time to waste. If she keeps criticizing and blaming, he doesn't have a chance. If I can explain to both of them how important it is that they change their behavior with one another, he may be able to do without a drink tonight. And maybe tomorrow night he could go to AA. We chatted for about fifteen minutes about how people treat each other when they don't get along, how much they try to control each other. I didn't use the term *external control,* but I set the stage for doing it when she joined us. When the bell chimed, I knew it was her. I walked out, introduced myself, and asked her to come in to talk. Tia is an attractive woman who looks competent, although I can't say exactly what it was that gave me that impression.

Doc: Tia, I'm glad you're here. If he's to stop drinking, he needs your help. But it's a two-way street; you need his help, too.

Tia: I've done all I can. I've put up with it for twenty years. This is the first time I haven't bailed him out.

Roger: She let me rot in that jail for two weeks.

Tia: I'm sorry. The court counselor told me it was the right thing to do.

Roger: But I could've lost my job.

Doc: Good, what you're doing right now is exactly what I want to talk about. Roger, I heard you blame her for you being left in jail. How is that going to help your marriage?

Roger: But she should've bailed me out.

Doc: It doesn't make any difference what she should have done. She did what she thought was right. You drove drunk because you thought it was right. So what? What you did and she did is over. None of us can change what we did a minute ago, much less what happened two weeks ago. Do you want to have a big fight about it? Is it worth getting drunk about?

They both looked at me. To them, that the past was over was a new idea. To bring home my point, I then said,

Doc: Go ahead. If you want to fight, do it. I won't interfere as long as you don't break anything or hit each other. Yell, scream, curse—do whatever you want.

Roger: I don't want to fight. That's all we do is fight.

Tia: Because all you do is drink. You expect me to stand up and cheer for the few days you're sober.

Doc: Tia, that's a good question. What do you think he expects you to do when he comes home sober?

Tia: Him come home sober? That's a joke. The few times he does, I get the feeling the son-of-a-bitch wants me to pin a medal on him.

Doc: Roger, is that what you want?

Roger: It's like what we talked about. She's after me all the time, whether I'm drunk or not. She let me have it all the way to work this morning. I was sober as a judge.

Tia: He's right. I can't help myself. When I think about all he's done to ruin my life, my kids' lives, his own life, I get furious. I'd have been better off this morning to keep my mouth shut, but I just couldn't do it.

Doc: No, not talking won't work either. It's better than fighting but not much better. He was sober. He's afraid of going to jail. You'd have been better off talking with him. Suppose this office was your car this morning. There he is, sitting in the passenger's seat, sober. Can you think of anything you might say to him that might help him with his problem.

Roger looked at her. That look was pleading for her to say something. While she was thinking, I asked him:

Doc: Roger, can you think of anything you would have liked her to say this morning that she didn't?

Tia: Good, that's good, Doc. I'd like a suggestion, I really would. I'm not being sarcastic. It's this morning. Here we are in the car. You're sober. Tell me what you'd like me to say to you?

Roger: It's not so much what I'd like you to say. It's mostly what I'd like you not to say.

Doc: Tia, Roger and I were talking about that before you came in. What do people who are upset with each other usually say to each other?

Tia: They complain; that's what I was doing all the way in the car this morning. When you're married to a drunk, what else is there to do?

Doc: Roger, tell her what we shouldn't do. Do you remember the words I said we shouldn't use if we are upset with another person?

Roger: Look, Tia. Don't get mad at me. . . . it's not my idea, it's his. I'm not sure I can remember it all, but he said, "Don't criticize, blame, complain, nag, threaten, and punish. And don't bail me out either, that's like a bribe." Enabling, that's what the Doc called it.

Tia: So, it's all my fault. That's impossible. I can't act like the blessed mother. My God, it's not only me; your own mother lets you have it whenever you talk to her.

Doc: Please be patient with me. I'm trying to teach you something totally new. I know it sounds crazy,

Tia, but give me a chance. Roger's right to this extent. But only this much. What comes out of your mouth is your fault. But that's all that's your fault. It's not your fault that he drinks, drives, and get's into trouble; that's his fault. What comes out of his mouth is his fault. If he loses his job, it's his fault. That's what we're here to work on. If you both keep doing the same thing you've been doing for twenty years, nothing will change. Nothing! Forget about whose fault it is. What could you have said to him in the car this morning that had nothing to do with criticizing, blaming, or complaining.

There was a very long pause.

Tia: Okay. I think I get what you mean. But it's easier here. I'm not angry like I was this morning. I might have said, "I'm glad you're sober. I hope you have a good day at work. I'll see you tonight in the doctor's office." How's that?

Doc: Roger, you're here with her in the car. She's just said what she said. What could you say to her?

Roger: I understand why you didn't bail me out. This is the first time in my life that I see how precarious my situation is. That two weeks in jail woke me up. And when you didn't yell at me all morning while you drove me to work, it felt wonderful.

Tia: That's the biggest bunch of drunken malarkey I've ever heard. I put up with you for years. You never ever came close to saying anything like that.

Doc: Malarkey or not, Tia, you've got to admit it's new. What you call malarkey, I call choice theory.

What you both do all the time to each other I call external control. Why come here if you both want to keep doing the same thing you've done for twenty years, maybe more each year?

Tia: What's choice theory?

Roger: Yeah, what are you talking about?

This is the first hopeful sign. Instead of sitting there aligned against each other, they are both together asking me what I'm talking about. Choice theory is powerful. That little skit in the car got their attention.

Doc: It's a new theory; it claims you choose essentially everything you do. Like you choose all the words that come out of your mouth. But even more important, it says that there are two ways to relate to each other. The one you've both been using since Roger got drunk for the second or third time is called external control psychology. I want you to give it up for a week. And replace it with choice theory. It could really help, and it could be fun.

Tia: But how can we do that? We don't even know what it is we're giving up—external control, was that it?

Roger: And replace it with choice theory. How do we do that?

Doc: It's like what you did in the car a few minutes ago. Do you want to try?

Roger: I'd like to try. (Tia nodded in agreement.)

Doc: I want you to read this little book together. Read it several times and see if you can do what it suggests. But both of you do it, not just one. It's called, *The Language of Choice Theory*. I'd like you to spend a week trying to use this language with each other at home. If you succeed, it'll be a totally different week than you've had in years, probably in your whole lives. Read it all—the introduction, everything. If you start having any trouble with each other, don't say what you were going to say. Grab the book before you go too far in the other direction.

Tia: Okay, I'll read the book, but answer me this. Right now he's sober, but what should I do if he goes to an AA meeting and comes home drunk. He's done that before. Or when he stays sober for a while, he's such a bear it's almost as bad as when he gets drunk. You don't know what he's like when he can't have a drink.

Doc: Okay, he's hard to live with. But you don't put up with it. What do you say when you get exasperated?

Roger: She nags, she threatens, she calls me a drunk. She says she regrets the day she married me. And a lot more I don't see any sense in repeating here. You get the picture.

Doc: Always the same?

Tia: Like playing back a tape.

Doc: Let me explain. You and Roger are both normal human beings. You got married for a normal human reason, you loved each other. But maybe I'm presuming too much. Did you love each other?

Tia: I loved him; I still do. I thought he loved me.

Roger: I still love you. I've never stopped loving you.

Tia: Okay, you still love me. Big deal. I've heard that song for twenty years.

Doc: As much as you love him and have stood by him, you've only used words and expressions to try to force him to change. That's external control. The more you play that tape, the more your relationship suffers. But what do you do, Roger, when she starts in?

Roger: I don't hit her. I feel like it, but I don't. I just walk out of the house. I want a drink so bad, I forget everything, and when I come home, she lets me have it again. But I'm so drunk, I don't even hear her. I just go to sleep.

Tia: But it's worse than that. Like I said, he's really a bear when he wants to drink but he's trying to resist it. He hangs around and complains about everything. The kids have learned to tune him out, but I can't. He blames me for everything. I can't even wash the dishes without him butting in and telling me how to do it.

Doc: See, that's exactly what I'm trying to teach you. All you're both doing is playing the same old tape. Doing all you can to control the other. I'm asking both of you to stop completely for a week. Read this book; your kids are old enough, read it with them if they're interested. The new stuff is choice theory. It's the opposite of external control. Choice theory brings people together. External control tears relationships apart.

Tia: Okay, so what do I do on the way home when he asks me to stop for a six pack? He'll say it's just a lousy six pack, but I'll tell you he knows how to get drunk. He'll get drunk on that.

Roger: I'm not going to ask you. I'll be okay.

Doc: I hope so, but if he does ask you, what would you say if you didn't want to start ranting and raving?

Tia: I should say, "I love you darling. I think you deserve a six pack." That would sure avoid an argument.

Doc: That's not as bad as you think. What you should say is, "Roger, by the time we left the doctor's office, we were getting along pretty well. Will drinking tonight help us to get along better?"

Tia: Oh, sure. And then he'll blow his top and accuse me of playing word games."

Doc: What'll you say, Roger, if she says that? Will you answer her question?

Roger: She'll never say that in a million years.

Tia: I think I know what the doctor's talking about. Let me ask you a question: Will reading that book help us to get along better, or should we just go home and fight like we always do?

Roger: Hell, Tia, we know how to fight. Let's go home and read the book. I'm not going to drink tonight; I don't want to stop for a six pack.

Doc: Roger, I'll see you next week. Tia can you get here like you did today? While I'm beginning to see Roger, I'd like all three of us to get together for the first month or two.

Roger: I'm going to check in with the AA guy tonight. The idea of going back to that jail, God, I'd rather be dead then spend a year there.

There is some efficacy in the legal usage of external control. The threat of going to jail was effective but only because Roger still has something to lose. If he goes to jail for a year, it may be too late. What I have to do is to take advantage of his fear and teach both of them choice theory. I've got the process started. They can't undo all the external control they've used for years; they can't undo anything. No one can. But they can start to give it up. If he attends some meetings, I'll bring up the idea that when AA works, it's because there's little external control in the process. But teaching choice theory is a tangible step beyond AA. It can do no harm and has the potential to do a lot of good.

15

Bob and Sue

It seemed to them that the slightest thing that displeased him could trigger a tantrum.

Every parent has a picture in his or her quality world of how a child should behave. It was her blatant disregard of that picture that caused Judith's parents to contact me. But Judith was sixteen, old enough to see me herself. Besides, her parents doubted they could do that much with her; they were happy I was willing to help out. But suppose she had been much younger, perhaps between starting to walk and preadolescence. Then, most of the time I would recommend that her parent or parents see me. She would not need be directly involved. This is not an ironclad rule; it's a guideline based on my experience. Each case has to be evaluated on it's own merits.

With children between preadolescence and about age thirteen, I work with both the children and their parents. Most children this age are still under enough parental control so that their parents could use the guidance to deal with them. With children aged fourteen and older, I stay in touch with their parents but rarely ask the parents to come for counseling. As Judith was, they are old enough to benefit from therapy themselves.

I believe that parents are by far the most important people in their children's lives up to about age fifteen, even if they don't get along well with the children. But after fifteen, most children who haven't followed their parents' direction for a long time stop listening seriously to what their parents have to say. If parents would use choice theory from the start, this might not happen as often as it does now. But as long as we live in a world dominated by external control, adolescents and parents are going to have a lot of conflict.

My skill is connecting. If I succeed, I can provide what my young clients need most: a good relationship with a responsible adult other than their parents. In this instance, *responsible* means that I will listen to their side of the story but I will also have the skill to persuade them to listen to my side, the adult side. It is from this relationship that I can help them to reconnect with their parents, no matter what their age. For years, almost half my practice was with young people aged fifteen to twenty. I kept in touch with their parents, but I always saw the young clients alone, and the experience was almost always successful.

Unfortunately, most adolescents who are not doing well tend to disconnect from their parents and turn to friends who are also disconnected from their parents. These birds of a feather very much flock together. While they get support from their peers, the support often takes the form of advising them to defy their parents, *exactly the kind of support they don't need*.

Sometimes they turn to adult relatives like grandparents, aunts, or uncles who may be able to connect with them enough so they can stay on good terms with their parents. But to connect with them, the relatives have to avoid trying to control them, which is difficult for external-control relatives in this situation to do. Finding a relative who knows choice theory would be fortunate, indeed. The same goes for teachers, ministers, family physicians, and school counselors, all of whom connect with adolescents and help many of them. In fact, any responsible adult who has the skill to connect with adolescents can be a great help.

Although this problem may not be clear when dealing with an adult, it is painfully apparent when dealing with a child: he or she starts to break the parent's rules. The younger the child, the more obvious this resistance is.

Bob and Sue were referred to me by their pediatrician, who sent me a note saying he was concerned about their son, Eric. Ever since Eric had turned one, he had been having tantrums that seemed to his parents to be far out of proportion to the provocation. Now at almost three, he would lash out at his parents and, even once in a while, at his year-old baby sister. It seemed to Bob and Sue that the slightest thing that displeased him—for example, if some food on his plate was wrong, his mother didn't come when he called, his teddy bear was missing, or someone had disturbed the arrangement of his toys—could trigger a tantrum. At times, it was difficult to figure out what the provocation was. Bob and Sue lived in dread of these outbursts.

Bob and Sue were a nice-looking couple in their early thirties, appeared devoted to each other, and were at their wits' end with Eric. The good part is that they didn't blame each other, so I didn't have to deal with that problem. Both worked, but they had an excellent baby-sitter who came early and took care of the children until they got home. The baby-sitter reported that with her, Eric was usually fine. If he did have an outburst, it didn't last very long. The tantrums were primarily aimed at the parents. It was ironic that because they worked, they tried especially hard to spend quality time with Eric. And the more they did, the more he seemed to want. They could count on him being good only if one or both of them literally devoted themselves to him alone.

After a short period of getting acquainted and hearing the foregoing information about the problem, I began by making the comment,

Doc: I can certainly see why you're here. You seem to be doing everything right, but nothing seems to work. I don't think I have to tell you that you've got a tough kid. Tell me, besides total attention when he wants it, is there anything at all that seems to work?

I want to assure them that although Eric is difficult, they are not at fault. Not that they're doing everything that would work with him, but they're both trying to do the right thing even if they have to bend over backward. What's wrong is they are dealing with a child who has discovered external control, who senses his parents are feeling guilty about leaving him with a caregiver all day and has become almost addicted to the power his tantrums give him to control them. When Eric is in charge, it feels very good, and he's in charge much of the time. And it's not that the parents are externally controlling; actually, it's just the opposite. They do, of course, try to control him, but it's not to force or dominate, just to try to calm things down and survive. As explained by choice theory, our needs vary in strength; some of us have a much stronger need for power than others, and Eric is one of those genetically power-driven people. This need for power doesn't mean that he will tantrum all his life. In fact, a strong need for power is a good prognosis for a productive life if he can learn to get along with people. This is the time to teach him; the longer he tantrums, the harder it will be for the people he needs to reach him. Although he is in control of his parents, he already senses that tantrums won't work with the woman who takes care of him during the day; she isn't nearly as concerned about him as are his parents. My job is to teach Bob and Sue how to deal with him, which means teaching them some of the more subtle differences between external control and choice theory.

Sue: Except for giving him total attention, nothing seems to work. But even then, any frustration, something so small I can't even figure out what it could be, can set him off.

Doc: Tell me what he does by himself. My experience with kids like him is that he does things on his own.

Bob: That's the funny part. He does a lot on his own; he plays with his dinosaurs for hours at a time. He has a long attention span, longer than most kids his age. We've talked to other parents; he's different from their kids in this way.

Sue: When he's having a tantrum, we sometimes just up and put him in his room. But we're reluctant to do it because he seems to like it. It's almost as if it's what he wants. He won't go in there on his own, but it's okay if we put him in.

Doc: Do you ever lose your temper? I mean really yell and threaten him?

Bob: We try not to, but sometimes we do. However, we don't hit him. We just try to hold him; he struggles, but after a while it seems to work.

Doc: This may sound crazy to you after all your difficulties with him, but I think he cares a lot about you, maybe more than you even want him to right now.

Sue: He has a very peculiar way of showing it.

Doc: Okay, I'll grant you that. But does he ever seem loving and enjoy being kissed and snuggled?

Bob: He's kind of like two people.

Sue: Like Jekyll and Hyde; we've talked about that.

Bob: There are times when he's superloving and he can't seem to get enough hugs and kisses; then there are the other times, the awful other times.

Doc: Do you ever try to give him a lot of love to try to abort a tantrum?

Sue: We do, we really do. And sometimes it works. If he's not too worked up, that's when it works.

Doc: How about punishing him? You don't hit him, which is very good. What else do you do?

Sue: We've tried all the usual things—taking away a toy or stopping him from watching television—but he just continues to tantrum or stares daggers at us and goes back to his dinosaurs. We'll never take those away. We tried doing that, and it was worse.

Doc: But even if putting him in his room isn't punishment, do you do it for a long-enough time, past when he may want to come out?

Bob: I don't think we've ever done that. When he seems to like it, we go get him.

Doc: I think there's where you're making the mistake. Putting him in his room may not be punishment; it may be what he wants, but that's fine. He won't ask you to do it because he senses you think it's punishment, so he's still in control when you put him in his room.

Sue: That's pretty sophisticated reasoning for a three year old.

Doc: It is, but look, he doesn't have anything else to do but try to control you. That's his present mission in life, and he's succeeding at it very well, or we wouldn't be talking together now. Besides there are times when he needs time off from you as much as you need it from him, so he still gets what he wants.

Bob: So what do we do?

Doc: You have to teach him that you have feelings, that you love him but your life doesn't revolve totally around him. As long as he's in control, as he is now, he'll never learn that lesson, and at three it's time he does.

Sue: But if we don't come in when he expects us to, won't he eventually start tantrumming in his room?

Bob: He may or he may not. It doesn't make any difference. If you leave him in there for longer than he expects, he'll get the idea. The point is, don't go in to get him out just because as soon as you put him in he stops crying. Leave him there for a few minutes. Then if he starts to cry, don't rush in to see what's wrong. Let him cry until he chooses to stop. That's when you should take him out. As soon as he detects that the rules of the game have changed, that you're not going to take him out immediately when he stops, after a few times he'll learn that he can't control you. He may start to scream again and keep it up for more than an hour. This may happen a few times, but he'll scream less and less each time.

Bob: Isn't there anything else we can do? I hate to just keep putting him in his room.

Doc: There may be, but nothing that's as effective. It's doing the same thing all the time that makes the point with a three-year-old. But look, all I can do is suggest and explain why. I can't tell you absolutely, but I think you'll have a much happier and more mature child if you take my advice. How is he with other children?

Sue: Mostly okay, but if he wants something and they won't give it to him, he get's aggressive. He pushes, but so far he hasn't hit or bitten them.

Bob: He's been getting better with other children; he loves his twice-a-week nursery school. The teachers like him a lot. He hasn't really lost it there at all.

At this point I have a lot of information that tells me that his outbursts are almost always against his parents whom he loves, who are terribly important to him but are also easily intimidated. Away from them, he's not so bad because he knows whom he can control and whom he can't. The problem is that he's figured out a self-destructive way to get their attention. And since it works, he has no real incentive to change. This is a subtle point and hard for his parents to see because as nice as they are, they are still external-control people. So when Eric acts up and then quickly quiets down in his room, they think they're now in control but they're not.

Doc: I have an idea for something I'd like you to try. But first, tell me, when you get home from work, either of you, and he's playing with his dinosaurs or some other toy or if he's watching television quietly, what do you do?

Bob: We say a prayer and leave him alone.

Doc: How about his little sister, do you leave her alone, too?

Sue: She's different. She's a mellow child. We usually pick her up and give her a hug, but she's happy just to see us. She isn't a problem.

Doc: She isn't a problem yet. She's watching every move you and he make. If you help Eric, she'll get a lot of help, too. When you come home, you don't get home at the same time, do you?

Bob: Different times; she gets home early, around four. I get home between six and seven.

Doc: Okay, when each of you gets home, walk right over to Eric and give him some attention. Try to do something he'd like that you haven't done before if you can think of anything. Go to him before he realizes he has to confirm his control over you. This is a preventive step. But after you give him a little attention, leave him alone. This strategy shows that you care but that you decide when you've given him enough attention. If he throws a tantrum, ask him to go to his room, but I don't think he'll throw one very often when you do this. It should help. But go further. Try not to think of putting him in his room as punishment. Say to yourself, *It's all I can do that has a good chance of working because it will.*

Sue: We don't do that now; it'll be different. If he's quiet, we leave him alone. I'm worried that doing what you suggest will rile him up.

Doc: It might. But mostly it won't. If you sense he wants to be left alone, just give him a kiss and let him be. But after a few minutes, go over and offer him some more attention. I think he'll have thought it over and then he'll want it. Kind of adjust it to him. You've been letting him alone until he tantrums. It's going to take time to break the pattern.

Bob: Do you really think this is going to work?

Doc: I do, but you pretty much have to do it like I suggested. Try it for a month; it can't make things worse. Then come back to see me. But I think in a month you may see some progress.

Bob and Sue were skeptical. They thought I was telling them to punish Eric more by keeping him in his room longer than he wanted and giving in to him more by offering the extra attention. But all I was suggesting was that they take the control away from him in both instances. It was a true negotiation; he'd get more and they'd get more. Right now it was all his way.

In about two weeks, I got a call from Sue. She said they were doing exactly as I suggested. Once in a while, they even brought something new home from work. Not a toy, not anything they bought, just something that might interest him—a catalog, a brochure, a picture, or a funny story from their day. She said it was working. They were also amazed at how quickly Eric learned that they were willing to put him in his room and keep him there until he stopped tantrumming—not just until he quieted down. It wasn't much longer, just enough to teach him they had feelings and needs, too. I told them to wait two more weeks and then come in. In the interim, I suggested that Sue buy the book, *Choice Theory*, and read Chapters One, Two, Three, and Nine. I didn't hear from Bob and Sue until they came in, but it was obvious things were better. They had the book with them.

Doc: I see you have the book. Do you understand what I'm trying to teach you?

Bob: We think so; we've read the book and talked about it a lot. You figured this theory out yourself?

Doc: I'm hardly the first. *Love thy neighbor as thyself* was way ahead of me. But don't love him so much that you let him push you around. I guess, I'm one of the first people to organize these ideas into a recognizable, teachable psychology. Tell me, what have you learned?

Sue: Eric is an expert in external control. He sure has the capacity to make me miserable.

Doc: Look, this is all new. It takes time to get acquainted with both external control and choice theory. You see, Eric hasn't made you miserable. No one can make you miserable. He chooses to be hard to deal with, and you choose your misery to deal with him. And at his age, it's up to you. He isn't going to help. It's hard to do, but from what you tell me, I think you're doing very well in your beginning use of choice theory. You feel better and, I'm sure, he feels better. When we choose anger or misery, it's always to try to control others or to control yourself. Young or old, it works the same way.

Bob: I kind of got that from book. But there's more, isn't there?

Doc: What's more is that it takes time. I've been practicing choice theory for years, and I'm still learning. My wife and I use it every day in our lives, and we're still learning. But why do you believe Eric is so much better?

Sue: It's those needs. He's able to satisfy them better when we give him this new kind of attention and not rush to take him out of his room when we have to put him in.

Doc: Does he need much more attention? Do you have to give him more than you used to?

Bob: Not really. Maybe more often but not nearly for as long a time.

Doc: That's typical. You'll catch on to how much he needs. It'll change from time to time. For a while he'll need less. But not too much less. When he's a teenager, he may need more. I know this doesn't have much to do with Eric, but I'm curious, do you argue much with each other? Are there any problems in your marriage?

Sue: We read that part of the book very carefully. We're trying some of that stuff. It's hard to do, but it seems to work.

Changing from external control to choice theory is basic to all I believe. Remember, if you are having difficulty in any relationship, that difficulty is caused by one or both parties using external control. When you replace external control with choice theory, things can't help but get better.

16

Roger and Tia

He wants you to love both him and his drinking.

Roger was only a few minutes late for his appointment. I noticed he was less nervous and better groomed than the last time I saw him. Even his clothes were neater and better pressed, as if he'd put some care into how he looked. Before I could say anything, he said with some enthusiasm: "Tia'll be here later. She wants to talk to you. But I'll tell you, we had quite a time with that book this week. It's the opposite of all we've been doing with each other for years."

"Tell me about it."

"First of all, I haven't gotten drunk. I've had a few beers, but I didn't overdo it. It's been a real good week."

This was typical. When he left last time, he said, "Nothing to drink." Now the first thing he tells me is that he's had a few beers. I can certainly see what Tia's upset about. I was tempted to call him on it, but it would have done no good—external control—and it might have jeopardized what little relationship we may have.

I said, "I'm curious, how many beers is a few?"

"A six pack for the whole week; that's hardly any at all. Tia didn't like it; she wants to talk with you about it. But, for me, it's damn good. I had no trouble stopping; that proves I'm not an alcoholic."

"Roger, like I told you, I'm not going to argue with you about whether or not you're an alcoholic. I'm not going to argue with you about anything. But don't let the fact that you've had a pretty good week go to your head. You've had good weeks before, lots of them. You wouldn't still have your job if you hadn't. But I'll tell you for you to stop drinking short of getting drunk is the same as stopping sex with an exciting partner before you're finished. Of course it can be done; once in a while anybody can do almost anything. But you've been picked up twice for DUI; your stopping ability is close to nonexistent. Look, I'm glad you had a good week. I'd like to hear about it."

I think it is important to hold a mirror up to a person I am counseling, especially an alcoholic who is still in denial. This was a good week for Roger. But true to form, he's focusing on the wrong thing: that he drank but didn't get drunk. That he didn't get drunk may have a lot more to do with the fact that he's still more scared of going to jail than anything else. But that fear will wear off; it never kept him sober in the past, and it won't now. What Roger needs to focus on is getting along better with his wife. Buying that six pack was going in the opposite direction.

He said, "On the way home we stopped in the bookstore and bought *The Language of Choice Theory.* Then we had to go to the market, and, okay, I did what I said I wouldn't do: I bought a six pack. Big deal; I felt like a beer. As soon as I put it in the cart, Tia didn't say what she said she'd say when we were here. She just looked daggers at me. She wanted me to put it back, but she didn't want to make a scene. All the way home from the market, she wouldn't talk to me; she was punishing me, I guess. I mean this's the way she's been for years. When she gets that way, all I can think of is, *I need something to drink*. Then when we got home, I got a bright idea. I said to her, 'You're ticked off about that lousy six pack. Let's read the book right now and see if we can learn something.' As soon as we got into it, I could see what was wrong. Doc, I've been through that market scene with Tia a thousand times. I buy some beer, and she stops talking and keeps giving me that look. So I say to myself, *Screw it!* and get drunk. The book's so short we started with the introduction and read it right through. You don't have to be a rocket scientist to see what you're getting at. There it was, our whole marriage, all external control."

"So what'd you do?"

"She said, 'Okay, I admit it. All I do is try to keep you from drinking. I'm terrified of that six pack. I can't help it; one six pack is how it always starts. Tell me, what do you want me to do that's better? We didn't see anything in that book that tells a wife how to talk to an alcoholic husband who's about to get drunk.' Doc, I thought about that and then I said to her, 'Okay, how about if you tell me something like this: Honey, I'm worried. We're barely home from the doctor, and you're ready to start drinking. But I've learned something. I'm even more worried about us living the way we've lived for years, arguing and fighting. I can live with you having two beers if we can get along better. Then, if it's all right with you, I'll take the other four out to the car and lock them in the trunk; you can get them tomorrow, If you'll accept that much, I think we can have a good night.'"

"You really said that? What happened?"

"She repeated almost everything I asked her to say. She was real calm; there was no look on her face. Then she pulled two beers out of the six pack and took the rest to the car. When she came back, I said, 'You didn't ask me if it's okay with me for you do that.' She said, 'I'm not willing to go that far. I gave you two beers; that's what you asked for. That's as far as I'm willing to go. If you want more, we'll have to go back to fighting. Here are the car keys; if you want, you go get 'em. But don't bring 'em back in here. Go drink them someplace else. If you drink more than those two beers in this house tonight, I'm going to tear that book into a million pieces.'"

"So what happened?"

"Nothing. I settled for the two beers. It's funny, I didn't even want anymore. And we did pretty well. We read the book again. We talked about it. I helped her to clean up; we even talked to our kids. Usually, as soon as they hear any kind of argument, they tune us out. But when they saw us having a good evening, they wanted to talk, too. And that's the way it has been all week. No more beer than that six pack—a bottle a day until I ran out. There's nothing to drink in the house now."

"Is that your new ration, one six pack a week? Are you going to stop for another one on the way home?"

"I've thought about it. But I don't think so. I want to see if we can have another good week without me drinking. I know that's what she wants. She'll tell you when she gets here. She really wants to talk with you."

"How about work?"

"Work was good, but I'll tell you, it was good because I didn't drink anything all week except those six beers. It's funny, I think the people who work for me know it when I'm not drinking. They treat me differently. I didn't get *that look* at the office either all week."

"But did you treat them differently; maybe this is what they noticed?"

"I guess I did. I didn't blow up as much. We got along pretty well. One of the guys, he's actually my best friend at work, asked me about it. I told him I feel better. My wife and I are getting along better. And that's the truth. He knows about my problems at home. It wasn't much, but we talked more this week than we've talked in years. We enjoyed it."

"How about the AA?"

"I went, I went to two meetings, four was too much. . . .

I interrupted, "Please, Roger, don't tell me how many meetings you go to. I've decided that's none of my business. It's between you and the judge. Coming here to see me once a week, that's my business. How'd the meetings go?"

"I don't think AA is going to work for me. I'll go and I'll listen; I don't want to go to jail. But four meetings a week is a lot of time to give up."

"Give up from what?"

When I asked that question, he knew what I meant: that

these meetings would cut into his drinking time or into his thinking-about-drinking time. He didn't say anything, and I just waited for his answer.

"Okay, I get what you mean. But when I sit there with all those drunks and listen to their drunken stories, all I think about is drinking."

This is a good example of alcoholic thinking. Almost everyone there is trying to stop, and he calls them drunks. And he blames his desire to drink on what goes on in the meetings.

"Do you think they all drink, that the meetings are a sham?"

"I don't know. It's like I told you, I sit there and I feel like drinking."

He doesn't want to answer that question. He's trying to escape from AA because he is surrounded by people just like himself who are trying to stop. As long as he wants to drink, it's an uncomfortable place to be. Four meetings a week are a lot for him to put up with. He even may be lying about going to two; maybe he didn't go to any or to only one. But that's between him and the court. I can't get any more involved in policing his actions than I am.

I said, "AA doesn't work for everyone, but for a guy like you who still has a wife and a family and a good job, it usually helps. But for it to work, people have to give it a chance."

"I'm going to go tonight. I'm going to stay for the whole meeting. And I'm going to go home cold sober like I came in."

That "Boy Scout" speech tells me he's still afraid of going to jail, and that's good. He was also looking for me to give him credit for going to an AA meeting. I don't want to do that any more than I want to criticize him for not going. AA is up to him. It's all up to him. He'll be perfectly willing to blame me for anything that happens if he screws up. I don't want him to be able to put me in that position.

"Those meetings you went to, they have a lot of regulars. Did anyone notice you were new?"

"Yeah, a couple of guys."

"Were they friendly?"

"I guess so, but more like insurance salesmen. Like I'm a client and they want to sell me an AA policy."

"How did it feel?"

"It felt okay. They were trying. They didn't push me to say anything. I liked that. Some guy got up and told a story about how drink'd messed up his life. Not an old guy either; I think he was in his forties. I'll tell you it was funny. I'm sure it wasn't funny at the time, but when he told it, it was really funny. It helped pass the time. Those meetings get long. Three a week; even that's too much. Do you think you could get that four cut down to three? I'm not drinking now. My wife needs me around more; the kids do, too."

Here he is, an alcoholic in all his glory. In a week he's already cured. And he's trying to give me credit for it, so I'll feel good and do him a favor.

"Roger, like I said, the meetings are between you and the judge; you'll have to talk to your probation officer. Has your wife said she'd like you to cut down? Oh, I just heard the bell, she's here; I can ask her myself."

"Please, don't ask her. She wants me to go four times; she thinks it's important. I don't want her to think I'm trying to con you. She's going to Al-Anon now; my old crap doesn't work anymore."

"Roger, there're no secrets here. I want to feel free to talk to Tia about anything. That's the way I conduct business. I'm not trying to control what you say, and please don't try to control what I say. . . . Do me a favor and go let her in."

Tia came in, and she, too, looked a little better. It's amazing how much a week without a drunken husband helps.

Doc: Roger told me about what happened this week. About the beer and how you read the book. He thinks it went very well; what do you think?

Tia: He's right, it was a good week. That book, it's so simple; we both like that. But it's no miracle.

We've had a lot of good weeks that never lasted. Fifty times he's told me this is the end of the problem. I want a good year; a good week doesn't mean a thing to me. For all I know, that book is just another short-term gimmick like going to a few AA meetings. Even seeing you, one session and bingo, he's cured. When I read that book with him, I said to myself, *Oh, oh here's another gimmick*. That's what I need to talk to you about.

Doc: I want to talk with you, too.

Roger: I think it's really going to work this time. I feel it.

I disregarded Roger. If I paid any attention to what he just said, I'd lose all credibility with her.

Doc: Tia, tell me what's on your mind. It's important that Roger hear what you say.

Roger: But we've never done what we did last week. We worked it out. That's different, very different.

Tia: Maybe, but if he hadn't had that beer, I'd be a lot more optimistic. I mean, he bought it right after we saw you. He gave me his one-little-six-pack smile; he seemed so happy. All I could think of is that nothing's changed. Do I have to keep living with, *Don't worry Tia, it's okay, just a few beers routine?*

Doc: Tia, do you think you'd have been better off if you'd taken a stand right there in the store, even made a scene?

Tia: I should have done something. If that choice theory you practice allows him to have beer, it won't work. You know that. Our kids know it. They're as worried about that beer as I am.

Roger: For God's sake, I won't drink any beer this week. I won't drink anything next week. . . . But once in a while, I need a beer. I handled it. I can do it again.

Doc: Roger, you beat the train to the crossing this time. Do you want to keep trying to beat it for the rest of your life?

Tia: That's a good way to put it. He won't even beat it the next time.

Roger: Shit. I do everything right. We have a good week, and then I get this.

We've gotten to the point where I have to make a move. And Tia has to help me. Roger's in total denial. But that's to be expected. I have to try to get both of them to take a new look at his drinking.

Doc: Roger, do you have any idea what the problem is?

Tia: It's Roger, he's the problem.

Doc: He's most of the problem but not all the problem. Tell me, Roger, what do you really want from Tia?

Roger: I want her the way she was this week—no arguments, no put-downs, no threats, and she let me have a six pack. It was a great week.

Doc: Tia, what do you think he wants from you?

Tia: That's a no-brainer; he wants me to let him drink.

Doc: That's right, but I think he wants even more than that. He wants what every alcoholic wants from his wife. He wants you to love both him and his drinking.

Roger: What are you talking about?

Doc: I'm talking about what you just said, "She let me have a six pack. It was a great week." Tia, that double love—love me and love my drinking—is what every alcoholic who comes in here wants. Are you willing to love his drinking? That's what he really wants.

Tia: No, never, never. . . . I hate his drinking. I can't stand it.

Doc: How about you, Roger? You had a great week because she let you have the beer. But think about it. How good a week would you have had if you couldn't have the beer?

Roger didn't answer for a moment. Then in kind of a lame way, he said, "I don't want her to love my drinking. *I* don't even love my drinking. I drink because I've got a disease; she shouldn't make a fuss every time I want a beer."

I ignored his attempt to change the subject. If it has any validity at all, the disease concept helps alcoholics to accept treatment; it does not provide an excuse to drink. This is the time to try to get to the core of helping him. I don't think there's any other way he can get help.

Doc: Roger, when you were in jail for that two weeks, what did you think about almost all the time?

Roger: Her, the kids, even my mother.

I kept looking at him.

Doc: Who else?

Roger: My job, the guys at work.

Doc: The people you drink with, did you really think that much about them?

Roger: No, not really. . . . Mostly it was Tia and the kids, my family.

Doc: How about drinking? Did you think a lot about getting drunk.

Tia: If he says he didn't think about drinking, I'm outta here.

Roger: I thought about it a lot. How much I'd like a beer or a little wine with my dinner. But that was at first. As the days went on, all I could think about were her visits. I wanted to hear about the kids; they wouldn't let the kids visit.

Doc: Do you know why you thought so much about Tia and the kids?

Roger: They're my family; they're all I have.

But they're not all he has. He also has alcohol. He's got to start thinking seriously that he'll lose all he has if he continues to drink. And keep all he has if he doesn't. How to get this across to him without threatening him (no external control) is not going to be easy.

Doc: Roger, this is not a simple question. Think about it; take your time. Why do you like to drink?

After a very short pause:

Roger: It feels so good. I don't understand why I have to give up that feeling.

Doc: When Tia visited you in jail and talked to you about the kids, did you feel good?

Roger: I felt good. I felt good whenever she came. It felt good just to see her.

Doc: How much is that feeling worth to you?

Roger: What do you mean?

Doc: Because it's that good feeling *or* the good feeling from drink. Unfair as it may seem, you can't have both. She will not love you and love your drinking. And your kids won't either.

Roger: I've got to tell you the truth. The first couple of times she visited, I was angry; I was pissed that she didn't bail me out. But I covered it up. I was terrified that she'd stop visiting.

Tia: Don't kid yourself that you covered it up. It was written all over your face. . . . But look, it was okay. I'm not in search of miracles. I'll tell you one thing, Roger, if you'd cussed me out for the whole time you were in jail, I still would've come to see you. I get no pleasure out of seeing you so miserable.

Roger: I knew that. I didn't stay angry very long. It may have done me some good to stay in jail.

This statement could be a con, or it may have a tinge of sincerity. I'll take it as a good sign. Why not? He isn't going to con me, and if she left him in jail, he isn't going to con Tia anymore either.

Doc: When she visited, did you ever worry she wouldn't take you back?

Roger: No, I knew she'd take me back. My going home, that's all we ever talked about.

Doc: Tia, can he count on you always to take him back? The next time he may be gone a year.

Roger: There's not going to be a next time.

Doc: Tia?

Tia: Not for me either. We got along fine while he was in jail. I've made up my mind. We don't need this anymore. Like you said, we love him, but we'll never love his drinking. If that's the price we have to pay to keep him, we're through paying it.

Doc: Roger, that's the story. It may not be the next time, but it'll happen. The real question is, How much do you need them?

Tia: He doesn't really need anyone when he's drinking. If they'd given him all the booze he wanted, he'd have been happy to stay in jail. If I've learned anything in twenty years, I've finally learned that.

Roger: It's not true; I need her. And when I'm drinking, maybe even more.

Tia: Sure. To bail you out, to cover up for you at work. All the things I did because I loved you. . . .

Then Tia paused and looked first at me and then at Roger.

Tia: My God . . . I was trying to love your drinking, too, wasn't I? I'll tell you Roger, right here in front of the doctor, if you bring anything to drink into the house again, we're through. Everything you own is going out on the front lawn with that bottle. But don't worry. I won't break that bottle. I know you need it more than you do me.

This was a dramatic moment. It's not often that the wife of an alcoholic gets through but I think she got through with this speech. It's no miracle, but it's a start. If Tia can continue to project that she means what she said and if Roger will continue to see me and go to AA, he has a chance.

Doc: Roger, you've got a choice. What do you think it is?

Roger: To drink or not to drink? That's been the question for twenty years.

Tia: What other choice does he have?

Doc: I wish it was that simple. It's a much harder choice than that.

Roger: I don't know what you're talking about. . . . I'm not good at riddles.

Doc: Well, answer this. Why don't you like to go to AA?

Tia: We've been over that a million times. He doesn't like it because he's with a lot of drunks.

Roger: Yeah, that's right, what good can those drunks do me?

Doc: No good at all if you think of them as drunks.

Roger: Well, that's what they are.

Doc: No, they're not. They're recovering alcoholics who are trying to continue their recovery. You don't want to be around them because they don't love your drinking anymore than Tia does. They go to those meetings to meet people like themselves who are also trying to recover—people who accept them, who won't put them down. They're trying to accept you, but you won't let them because they won't accept your drinking.

Roger: The hell with them; I don't need any of them.

That's enough about AA. I know I got through to him because of how angry he got. But that's enough for this week; it's time to wind it up. But I don't want to leave him feeling angry.

Doc: I think we've had a real good get-together. I look forward to seeing both of you again next week.

Roger: Tia, did you mean it? No more drink in the house at all?

Good! that registered on Roger.

Tia: Roger, we've been over the house and garage with a fine-tooth comb. There's not a drop to drink; we even threw out the vanilla extract. If we find anything else, you're out. I hope you think I'm serious. Please don't give me that surprised act if it happens.

That was reality. It may have been the first time she stood up for herself and her kids and meant it.

Doc: What's the plan for this coming week?

Roger: The same as this but without the booze. With them all looking at me, drinking at home was a bummer anyway.

Roger and Tia left arm-in-arm. It's always amazing to me how quickly alcoholics can shift back and forth from being angry to being lovey-dovey. I guess it's how they manage to keep the few connections they have. The rest of my counseling with him will depend on doing more of what I began today: Working to get him to realize that, literally, his life depends on keeping his family connections.

He can't just stop drinking; he's done that a thousand times. This is a goal no counselor can achieve. In fact, no one can counsel anyone to stop anything. He can no more stop wanting to drink than an overweight person can stop wanting to eat. All either can do is find some other behavior that works better. That's where I'll continue to focus with Roger and with Tia. I'll begin to counsel him toward improving the best thing he has: his family relationships. And maybe start something new at work that will help him get along better with the people there.

Less than a week ago, Tia and Roger were totally external control with each other. Now they've also experienced a little choice theory. Even though it was for the wrong reason, that speech he made up for her to say was impressive. He'd learned something, and she appreciated it. Even with the beer, she admitted they'd had a good week. As they continue to see me, they'll learn a lot more choice theory.

As I said before I saw him the first time, drinking is a classic control issue. Alcoholics drink to get the feeling that they've escaped the control of others, and the more they drink, the more they lose control over their lives, as Roger did when he was put in jail. Tia, on the other hand, gained control when she didn't bail him out. She may have been serious when she said, "No more drink at home"; I hope so. A large part of why reality therapy works is that it gives alcoholics a respite from external control.

17

Jerry and Carol

I'm asking you to be more sensitive to my needs than a man has a right to ask a woman.

Two weeks after our last meeting, Jerry sent me the following brief manuscript, along with a note saying he'd be waiting to hear from me. In the note he said that what he'd written wouldn't make sense to anyone except me and Carol, so would I please not judge it as if I were a stranger reading it for the first time.

Working It Out Together

Jerry B.

Carol saw something in Jerry that no one else seemed to see. Although he was crazily compulsive and occasionally hostile, for the two months she'd known him, he was never that way toward her. She'd met him at a Directors Guild preview of the film *As Good As It Gets*. An actress who was one of Carol's clients—she went to the homes of wealthy women to make them up before they went out—had given her the ticket. She was both appalled by and strongly attracted to the film's main character, Melvin Udall. Nasty as he was, as the film progressed, she became more and more enthralled. This man had a reservoir of untapped love.

When she got up to leave there were tears in her eyes. As she was walking out, she was pushed against a huge man; Carol is petite, barely five feet tall. He immediately turned to her and excused himself for bumping into her even though it was she who had bumped into him. As he looked down at her to apologize, they both saw tears in each other's eyes. All around them people were laughing and making cracks about the nastiness of Melvin Udall, here was a man who for some unknown reason saw him the same way she did. Carol had connected with Jerry.

They spent the next two hours talking nonstop to each other in a nearby coffee shop. Before that evening was over they learned a lot about each other. Jerry was as crazy as Melvin. So crazy he carried his own silverware around in a little case; he wouldn't use the restaurant spoon to stir his coffee. He told her that if she cried for the man in the movie, she should feel free to cry an ocean for him. He could match Jerry's craziness compulsion for compulsion, obsession for obsession, and even go Melvin at least one compulsion better.

But Melvin was an actor playing a sensitive man, Jerry's sensitivity was real; it was apparent from the time she bumped into him and he looked down at her to apologize. His sensitivity continued in every detail of that first conversation they shared. Jerry could match Melvin's sensitivity, tear for tear and go him a few tears better. If she was willing to put up with his craziness, he assured her, she'd found a man who would unlock fifty-five years of pent-up love into every part of her life. At the end of their first meeting, she was willing to take a chance on him.

At the department store in which she sold makeup, she told her friends about the movie but not about her attraction to Melvin and her meeting with Jerry. When it came out, they all saw it and enjoyed it but no one came close to seeing in Melvin what she'd seen so strongly.

They all told her it was fantasy. The heroine in the movie was out of her mind to even give him the time of day, much less fall in love with him. Melvin was a beast that no beauty could transform. She didn't breathe a word to them about Jerry.

She then went on a trip with him to Santa Barbara to see her daughter, Jill, a college student. Jill told her be wary. A man who had to wash his hands all day long was hardly someone she should get involved with. She'd told her daughter all about him the night they were together in the dorm. Jerry stayed in a nearby motel. Jill said, "Mom, you're a beautiful woman, get a normal man for a change instead of a carbon copy of that crazy Melvin Udall."

Even his next-door neighbors who had known him for twenty years took her aside the night they all got together for a party and warned her to be very careful; she ought to see the crazy way he walked when he went out to get the paper or the mail, two steps forward, one step backward. The only one who supported him was Blaze, the cat next door—actually the neighbor's cat in theory but Jerry's in practice. The cat loved Jerry and soon loved Carol. He told her that any man who bought him six-dollars-a-pound fish for dinner was a man worth serious consideration. Jerry was well-off; while cats may also be romantic, they never lose sight of the practical side of any relationship.

What she did was combine the cat's pragmatism with her romanticism and decide to keep giving him a chance. That first night, as a test, she'd told him briefly about her abusive husband. He had to be sensitive to her fear of sexual involvement, and she was surprised at his total sensitivity in that area. After two months it had gotten to the point where she began to feel she might have overstated her case. She wanted more, not much more, but a little more than to be held. A single kiss was as far as he would go beyond holding her and rubbing her back.

And she sensed that he was frightened when their lips touched briefly as if that little bit more might be too much.

Now she began to fantasize about the heroine in *As Good As It Gets*, who has come out on a rainy night in a wet T-shirt without a bra on to tell Melvin that just because he was paying for a doctor for her sick child, he shouldn't get any ideas that she'd give him sex in return. More and more Carol kept thinking, *I wish I could be that girl in the wet shirt with Jerry. He's totally familiar with my back, I'd like him to get a little more acquainted with my front.* But that fantasy she kept to herself. The idea of sharing it with Jerry was more than she was ready for. For years in her marriage she'd had sex without love. Now she was in the opposite situation, love without sex. It was good, very good, but she could no longer deny the truth: She wanted more.

But in the past month, when her sexual feelings for him began to grow, he seemed sad each time they got together. But then, after a few minutes, the sadness would disappear. It wasn't enough for her to ask him about it, but it was there. And it continued even though he told her on several occasions that his writing was going well, he loved her very much, and had no intention of ever saying or doing anything that had the least chance of hurting her. The last time he said that he emphasized, "I will never hurt you, ever."

This reassured her, and she tried not to think about the sadness. But she was right about it, it was there, because one evening when they were sitting together on his sofa, she often came for dinner, he brought it up.

"Have you noticed I'm a little sad when we get together but then it clears up? You must have noticed, I can't seem to hide it."

Carol said she had noticed it and she didn't understand it. But since the sadness cleared up quickly, she'd decided not to worry about it. But she was pleased he was sensitive enough to bring it up and said, "Will you tell me about it? If I can, I'd like to try to help."

"This is very difficult for me. But I have to tell you the truth. I'm sure you know I love you. You do know that, don't you?

Carol squeezed his hand when he asked that question. He continued, "I need your help very much. If I thought I could deal with this myself, I'd never have brought it up."

They'd been holding each other close when he began to tell her, and he could feel her heart jump in her chest when he asked her for help. She was puzzled, help with what? What could be wrong. Then he said,

"Remember the night in the movie when Karen, the woman Melvin had befriended came to his house in the wet T-shirt. All I can think of when I'm with you is how much I'd like to see you in a wet T-shirt. That fantasy is driving me crazy. Please don't reject me—I had to tell you. I had to tell you how I feel. For the past month, I could sense you trusted me completely and now you'd like to make love. I've been sad when I'm with you because I'm afraid you'll say something about wanting to. When you don't, I relax. But tonight I'm not sad. I made up my mind I was going to have this talk with you. Would you talk with me about it?"

Carol thought hard for a minute. She wondered why he was sad at first, as if he was afraid she was going to suggest something he couldn't handle and then he relaxed when she didn't. It was just the opposite of what she expected him to say. But then she said,

"Jerry, I'll talk with you about anything. If there's any reason you haven't pushed for sex, I'll respect it. I'll respect anything you do or don't do, darling, because you respect me. It's hard for a woman to get respect in this city, for a woman like me who's been abused and needs extra sensitivity it's almost impossible. You've changed your whole life because of me. Do you know how much I appreciate that? I think about it all the time. If you have some problem with sex, I won't put any pressure on you. There's a lot more to love then sex. I've never come close to getting from any man what you give me every day. I love you very much."

"Carol, I want to make love to you. I want it more than anything in the world right now. But I'm afraid. I'm afraid I won't be able to do it. This may be hard for you to believe, but I've really never done it with anyone I care for in my whole life. The few times in my life that I've met a woman I feel something for I'd crank up my craziness and it was all over. I'd use my craziness to reject them before they rejected me. I cared for you the night I met you more than I've cared for any woman in my life. I'm asking you to be more sensitive to my needs than a man has a right to ask a woman. I'm not crazy anymore; I'll never be crazy again as long as I have you. Be patient with me, that's all I ask."

After they exchanged their feelings, they just stayed together on the couch wrapped in each other's arms. Jerry said, "Carol, may I touch your breasts?"

Now Carol was nervous. She could sense he wanted to try to go a little further, and she didn't want him to fail. But she didn't want him to feel she was putting any pressure on him to succeed. She thought the best thing was not to do anything except say one word,

"Please."

Very slowly he lifted her blouse and unhooked her bra. She just lay there as he very gently caressed her breasts. This is what she'd been wanting for weeks, and it was all she could do to lie still. She was tempted to do more but she restrained herself. What was the hurry? He needed time. It had taken him weeks to get this far. She said to herself, *Carol, relax, don't break this mood.* He went from caressing them to kissing them and nibbling gently on her nipples. She began to shudder and had a huge desire to reach down and touch him. But she didn't. She was delighted. She could sense his growing excitement. Then, slowly and gently as if this were almost a religious ritual, Jerry pulled her blouse down and said, "Can you get away this weekend?"

Carol almost said, "I can, I've got time coming." The few times in her life that she'd felt loved she'd been an enthuiastic partner. God, to spend a weekend making love with him! But caution prevailed. She said only, "Tell me about this weekend."

"I don't want to try to do anything more here, now. If we're going to make love, I want to do it in a new place. Not here, not at your place, a romantic place like I write about in my scripts. I've made a reservation for this weekend at the Bel Air Hotel, it's the most romantic hotel in town. I'd like to check in Friday night and spend the weekend with you. Carol, I want to be able to go slow. Even if I'm not able to do it I want to try. It would be a start if not a finish."

For a man who'd never written a word about sex, that scene in which he kissed her breasts was a huge step forward. As I read what he wrote, I appreciated his sensitivity to what she must be going through with him. This same sensitivity must be apparent in his scripts or he would never have sold one.

As I thought about what he'd written for me, I could now see how difficult an assignment I'd given him. But still, he'd come through. I was perfectly willing to agree that if he'd like to share this piece with Carol, I'd say it was a good idea. Jerry came in the next day. I could see he looked tense, he was very concerned about what I thought about what he'd written. I told the truth: "It's good Jerry. Very good. It's exactly what I'd hoped for. Would you tell me how you felt when you wrote it?"

"It didn't come easy. What you read is the third version. The others were so far off base I'd be ashamed to show them to you. But the picture of her in that wet T-shirt stuck in my mind. And I just had the idea that it may be on Carol's mind, too. After I thought about that, the rest came easy because it was the truth . . . . Okay, I wrote it, it's good, now what?"

"I think you should produce it. Cast yourself as Jerry and I think Carol could play the female lead perfectly. She wouldn't even have to change her name. How'd you come up with those names? It was a stroke of genius."

"Okay, okay! if I want a comedian I'll watch Comedy Central."

"I'm sorry. I'll be serious."

"Doctor, the first time I saw you, I mean before you knew about my sex problem, I asked you why I'm the way I am. And you didn't give a crap about my childhood, you said, "It's gone. Your problem is now." That's been bothering me. There's got to be a reason for the way I am. I don't think I was born this way. Psychiatrists help people like me to figure out the reasons. If I could do it on my own, I wouldn't need you."

"No, you weren't born this way. And you're right, there is a reason you're this way. There's a reason for every behavior we choose as there's a reason for every word you write. There is a reason you're afraid of sex. And it isn't because you had a few visits with prostitutes. You were afraid of sex before you ever saw them. All you got from them is an excuse not to have sex anymore."

"See, I told you there was a reason."

"Jerry, it's a lot more than that. I don't know what it is. I really don't. No one knows. People are complicated. We can't always figure out the reason for the things they do or can't do. . . . But let's say I work with you for a long time and we figure out the reason. We really know it. . . . Say your mother rejected you when you were young, she gave her love to your father or to other men. You learned that women can't be trusted, to steer clear of them so they won't reject you. Then to go further, you reject them before they reject you by showing them your craziness. That's a very standard story. I'll bet a million clients have worked that one out with their therapists over the past hundred years."

"Well, to some extent that was my story. My father left when I was five, I never saw him again. He was killed in the war. My mother had a lot of boyfriends but she never remarried. I was jealous of them but she never rejected me. I loved her; she did the best she could."

"Okay, I'll go with that. You wanted more from your mother than she gave you. It's not quite rejection but, when you were young, you might have seen it that way. So what do you want to do about it now? You want to reject Carol before she rejects you?"

There was a long pause as he realized the fallacy of blaming his mother. Really blaming anyone. If she was at fault or he thought she was, either way, what could he do with that information now?

"I don't want to reject Carol."

"So don't. What's stopping you from accepting her? If you want to distrust women for the rest of your life, I can't help you. Psychiatry is not magic; it can't fix the past. Nothing can fix the past. You have to give it up. It's over, Jerry. It's only alive if you choose to keep it alive. Or if you're so afraid of the present that you want to hide in the past. Nothing may have happened in the past. All we really know is that you're the way you are now. That's all we can work with; if you want to revisit the past, you'll have to find someone else to help you do it.

There was another long pause. Then he said, "I'm scared I'm going to blow it with Carol."

"Of course you're scared. But that fear is right now, it's not in the past. Did you really make a reservation at the Bel Air Hotel?

"No, but I checked the suites out."

"Were you scared when you looked at the suite?"

"A little at first. But then it got to be fun. I felt good. I wonder, should I show what I wrote to Carol?"

"Is there any reason not to show it to her? It's the truth, isn't it?"

"But that part about her breasts, won't she be offended?"

"Were you worried she'd be offended when you wrote it?"

"No. But I get carried away a little when I write. I think most writers do."

"It was pretty sexual for you; did you feel upset when you wrote it?"

"No, I felt fine."

Actually, I thought it was progress that Jerry was able to express himself sexually and wanted to show it to Carol.

"Go with how you feel. She cares about you. I can't believe she'll be offended. Are you going to see her tonight?

He nodded.

"Why don't you read it to her? Tell her it was your homework assignment from me. I think she'd enjoy that. Then when we see each other next week, we'll talk."

"I've been thinking about something else. I feel pretty good. How long do you think I'll have to see you?"

"Jerry, I'm happy you feel better. But I'd like to keep seeing you until you work things out with Carol."

"You really think I'll work things out with her?"

"I think so. But I'm far from sure. Jerry, you're trying to change the way you live your life, there's still a way to go. Besides I enjoy seeing you, I look forward to it."

He agreed to continue to see me. He knows he still has the problem of making love to her. I think what he wrote is good, but no one can predict what'll happen. If things don't work out, I want to be there to help him from going off the deep end. In what he wrote he may have given Carol credit for patience and understanding she may not have. He shouldn't be on his own right now.

The next morning, I got an urgent call from Jerry, he wanted to see me right away. I was able to change my schedule enough to work him in at one. When I opened the door to the waiting room I was surprised to see a woman with him. He quickly introduced us and said, "Carol wanted to see both of us; this couldn't wait."

By the time we got into the office Carol was already talking:

Carol: You know about what Jerry wrote, he told me he wrote it at your suggestion.

Doc: That's right, he did. He asked me if he should show it to you and I could see no reason not to. But Carol, he wrote it; I had nothing to do with what he said. I didn't ask him to change a word.

Carol: Oh, I have no problem with what he wrote. It's actually quite romantic. But when I read it, I felt as if I were being set up.

Jerry: "Set up." That's what she told me. I don't understand and she won't explain. She just said she wanted to come here with me to see you.

Carol: I love Jerry. I can't bear the idea of losing him. Doctor, it's just like he wrote, he respects me, he really does. Do you have any idea what being respected by a man I care for means to me?

I nodded and she continued.

Carol: I'm forty years old. In my whole life, the only adult who loves me and respects me is my mother. I was never respected by a man, any man, least of all Jill's father. That drunk abused me for years and from the time Jill was a baby he abused her, too. I don't want to go into this in depth, Jerry can tell you about it if you're interested. Well, finally, after twenty years, he was killed in a car accident; Jerry told you about it. He had no insurance and I was wiped out. That happened two years ago. Before I met Jerry, just the idea of getting involved with another man made me sick to my stomach. Then along comes Jerry. Well, you know that story, too. I don't know what happened to him but, can you believe this, it was immediately apparent to me that he's even more desperate for love than I am. At least, that's the way I see it. So he's afraid of sex, big deal. To me it's a plus not a minus. He loves me and respects me, that's what counts for me.

Jerry: I do, darling, I do. I'm sorry I wrote that stuff about your breasts.

Carol: No, no, that was fine. I'm glad you wrote it. You asked for permission, it's another sign of your respect. You can touch my breasts anytime you want. What I'm upset about is the romantic weekend in the hotel. I don't want to go. I'm afraid to go. Don't you see why, Doctor? Help me to explain it to Jerry.

Doc: I'm not sure I see why.

Carol: Jerry's not ready. He's not even close to being ready to expose himself to a weekend in that hotel. I'm not a doctor but I know as soon as we get into that must-succeed situation he has a good chance of failing. Men don't do well when there's pressure on them to perform. The man I was married to beat me up when he couldn't perform, the son of a bitch blamed it on me. Jerry'll never do that but the end of that story is too pat, too orchestrated, too much like a fairy tale. It has a romantic ending that may not happen.

Jerry: But I said, it'd just be a start.

Carol: When men start something sexual, they expect to finish and they tend to be seriously disappointed if they can't. . . . And they look for blame. . . . And I'm going to be blamed. I'm being asked to do something that I'm almost sure is going to hurt us. . . . Doctor, I want you to explain to Jerry what I'm talking about.

Doc: You explain it, Carol. I think you're doing a better job than I could.

Carol: Is it okay, Jerry, if I tell you what's wrong? I hope you'll agree with me, but I have to tell you what's on my mind.

Jerry: Please, please tell me.

Carol: It's that piece you wrote. It was beautiful. Jerry, you're so romantic but I feel I have to protect both of us from your romantic notions. A suite at the Bel Air Hotel, a thousand bucks a night, how could I deal with the pressure of that situation? I don't want anything set up at all. In movies the lovers all do it easily, or it's strongly suggested they succeed. Sex is easy, there're never any problems. But this is real life; people fail a lot in real life, especially if you've never really done it before. Honey, you don't need any additional pressure. I love you, darling. I love every minute we're together. You don't have to do anything more for me than just be there and hold me close. Let's be careful. Let's not get into any situation where either of us may fail. It'll change everything. In what you wrote, kissing me and caressing my breasts, I loved it. You did it because you wanted to, not because you felt obligated to go further. Going to a hotel with an agenda is artificial. I don't think it'd work.

Carol showed a depth of feeling and understanding that was extraordinary. As she talked I could see him catch on. The romantic weekend in the hotel that seemed so sensible when he wrote it was so wrong as she explained it. I agreed with her. Why take any chances? He's found Carol; she recognizes what he needs. She's right, there's no hurry.

Jerry: She's right, Doctor. I was worried about that weekend when I wrote it. Blame it on the writer in me. If it weren't for Carol, that romantic fool could get me in a lot of trouble. There's no hurry. Our time will come. When it does we'll both know it.

Carol: We will. I felt more love last night in your soft caresses than I can't remember when.

Jerry took her into his arms and hugged her. There were tears in his eyes and she was sobbing. I was tearful too.

Doc: Carol, I asked Jerry to keep seeing me because I was almost sure there were still going to be problems. But now I'm a lot less concerned. You just handled a big problem, he's lucky to have you. If he'd come to me with the problem of your not wanting to go to the hotel, I don't think I'd have figured it out. It makes so much sense now that you've explained it. I appreciate your coming here. If it's okay with Jerry, I'd like you to feel free to come in with him anytime.

They left. There was nothing for me to say. Male sexual failure is almost always connected to expectations. She recognized the trap. That's why she felt set up. In my experience the greatest teachers of psychotherapy are clients. Carol taught me something I'll remember for the rest of my life. But I also think it was good for him to write what he wrote, and it was good for her to read it. He may have flunked the ending, but the rest of it held up well. It showed his sensitivity and his desire to love and respect her.

Over the next several months I continued seeing them whenever they called for an appointment. Things worked out remarkably well for Jerry and Carol. There's nothing more to tell.

18

Final Comments

We still need what we needed thirty-five years ago: better, quicker, more understandable, teachable psychotherapy to replace ineffective traditional therapy.

What distinguished the original *Reality Therapy* thirty-five years ago from other books of its time was my emphasis on responsibility: specifically, we are responsible for all we do. Much of what I was doing then was working with delinquents and students who were failing in school. Most readers had no problem accepting that these young people were responsible for their actions. In fact, this idea was considered a step forward in working with them. But I also claimed that we were responsible for what was then, and still is, labeled mental illness. Many readers had, and still have, difficulty accepting this responsibility.

In my 1998 book *Choice Theory*, the theory I use throughout this book, I expanded my claim that we are not only responsible for delinquent behaviors, school failure, and mental illness, but that we actually choose these behaviors. In fact, I now believe that *we choose essentially all we do*. To explain this theory, I have created the concept of total behavior to expand and clarify what behavior actually is. For example, total behavior answers the objections of people who tell me, "I'm depressed; no one in his or her right mind would choose to feel the way I feel." But when they are taught choice theory, they learn that they do choose to depress. They also learn that they can make better choices—a hopeful idea that most clients welcome.

Total behavior explains that all behavior is chosen and is made up of four *inseparable* components: *acting, thinking, feeling,* and *physiology*. This concept explains that we can only directly choose our actions and thoughts. But we have indirect control over most of our feelings and some of our physiology. However, the actions and thoughts we choose are inseparable from the feelings and physiology that go with them. The clients I counseled in this book, almost all of whom felt bad, learned in therapy to choose more need-satisfying actions and thoughts as two of the four components of a much more effective total behavior.

But then people ask, if we choose all we think and understand, how do you explain hallucinations and delusions? These are disorders of thinking and perception. To deal with that question, I explained that there is a large amount of creativity in almost every important total behavior we choose. Triggered by frustration, creativity works continually in our brain and is capable of offering us newly created actions, thoughts or perceptions, feelings and physiology. But since these components are connected, any change in one is the source of a new total behavior.

In most instances, we accept what is offered but then, later, may reject this new total behavior when we figure out more satisfying actions and thoughts. Rebecca, who hallucinated, was able to turn off these false perceptions when I helped her to deal with the conflict that caused them in the first place.

In *Choice Theory*, I expanded the two needs, love and worth, of the original *Reality Therapy* to five needs, *survival, love and belonging, power, freedom,* and *fun*. To satisfy these needs, I believe we create a simulated world in our brain in which we store memories of all our strongly pleasurable experiences, along with knowledge of additional pleasure we would like to experience. I call this world, the quality world. The quality world is specific; it is what we want to satisfy our needs. It is the source of all our motivation, literally, the core of our lives. I used this concept specifically in the case of George, but I have actually used it in every case I have counseled.

I have replaced my use of the term *responsibility* with the more explicit idea that we *choose* all our behavior because we can't be anything but responsible for all we choose to do. This way, I avoid any possible argument over what is responsible and what is not.

From the beginning of therapy with any client, the therapist looks for what I believe is always wrong: that the client, using external control psychology, is not able to establish the satisfying relationships he or she needs. The goal of therapy is to help clients establish these necessary relationships.

To do so, the therapist tries to create a satisfying relationship with clients and from this relationship, teach them to connect with others in their lives. In doing reality therapy, the therapist continually asks clients to evaluate the effectiveness of what they are choosing to do. And to see if it is possible for them to make better choices to get what they want: what is pictured in their quality worlds.

Finally, the therapist looks for every opportunity to teach choice theory to clients and their families so that everyone involved can begin the process of replacing external control psychology with choice theory.

In Chapter Two of the original *Reality Therapy*, I contrasted reality therapy with what I then called traditional psychotherapy. Based mostly on Freud's work in psychoanalysis, traditional therapy emphasized that people who need therapy are (1) mentally ill, (2) suffering from childhood trauma that led to unconscious conflicts, (3) able to understand their conflicts only by reliving them in therapy, and (4) displacing their conflicts onto the therapist through a mysterious process called transference.

Traditionally, mentally ill clients (1) are seen as helpless to stop doing, thinking, and feeling whatever constitutes their mental illness; (2) have no responsibility for their behavior, which is beyond their control; and (3) can be helped only by giving them insight into the whole process, although they must figure out how to use that insight to help themselves.

Traditional therapy, even if it is not psychoanalysis, is a long, time-consuming process that does not usually have a predictable, satisfactory result. For more information on the difference between traditional therapy and reality therapy, I suggest that you read Chapter Two of *Reality Therapy*. That 1965 chapter is as accurate today as the day I wrote it.

But even though many critics of traditional therapy say it is too long and unfocused to be as effective as it should be, at least it is going in the right direction: talking to people who are unhappy and trying to help them figure out how to improve their lives.

Today, we are facing a far more serious obstacle to psychotherapy itself, regardless of how quick and effective it may be. Increasingly, psychiatrists, still the leaders in mental health, are giving up on psychotherapy altogether.

Most psychiatrists today, who do not do psychotherapy, would claim that all the clients I counseled in this book were suffering from some variety of mental illness caused by some sort of a neurochemical imbalance in their brains. They have concluded that because these clients' brain chemicals are out of balance, it is worthless to talk with the clients. What these people need are brain drugs to correct their abnormal brain chemistries. And once their brain chemistries are corrected, they will be cured and able to resume normal lives.

Psychiatry has moved in this direction for several reasons. The primary reason is economic: Traditional psychotherapy takes too long and is too expensive. If the problem is a mental illness, then brain drugs are the obvious answer. The claim is that drugs are sure, quick, and less expensive than hours spent with a traditional therapist who can't or won't predict a desirable outcome in a reasonable amount of time.

Another reason is that a psychiatrist, who has invested in at least twelve years of training, including medical school, cannot make a living doing psychotherapy. Few clients could afford what he or she would have to charge. And fewer health plans would pay for it. But in the new managed care environment, which is more and more the way all mental health care is delivered, only a psychiatrist can diagnose and treat mental illnesses. Psychiatrists make careers of diagnosing mental illness, prescribing drugs, and supervising patients who take them. Many see psychotherapy as competition for mental health dollars.

But another huge reason for this movement away from psychotherapy is that there are billions of dollars to be made from psychiatric drugs. Since these drugs can rarely change the way clients choose to live their lives, they tend to be needed for long periods. And like all such nonspecific drugs, they tend to work less well over time. But if one drug doesn't work or continue to work as it should, the answer is a new drug—a no-lose proposition for the pharmaceutical companies. Since our society will never run out of disconnected people and as long as we believe in mental illness, the industry will never stop producing new drugs to treat it.

Furthermore, there is still a widespread idea among almost all people that if someone feels bad, he or she is not responsible for this feeling. But they believe that the pain, for example, the pain of clinical depression, is treatable with a drug. Diagnosing these choices as mental illnesses and treating them with drugs is a relief to all involved: the patient, psychiatrist, insurance carrier, and drug company: a four-party marriage made in heaven. The human desire to escape responsibility for what we choose to do is alive and well in all parties to this process.

When you ask many psychiatrists what is causing the present fixation on imbalanced brain chemistry, they go full circle and return to traditional beliefs: that trauma in childhood and/or traumatic adult experiences are the cause. But instead of trying to counsel these unhappy disconnected people, they claim that the trauma has caused the brain chemistry to go awry and that it must be fixed with drugs. They believe that psychotherapy, by itself, is ineffective. What we have is the old wine (trauma) in new bottles (medication).

What I am trying to point out in this book is that we don't need to spend so much money on expensive drugs. In many instances, as was shown in this book, no drugs were needed at all. But what is more important is that these drugs may be toxic to our brains. To quote from Dr. Peter R. Breggin's book *Toxic Psychiatry*, "Psychiatric drugs and electric shock are spreading an epidemic of permanent brain damage."

Reality therapy, as explained in this book, is what I offer. But I also think we have to go beyond therapy and focus on prevention by teaching people who are unhappy to give up external control and replace it with choice theory. Such teaching can be done in large groups at a low cost by well-trained mental health paraprofessionals. It is teaching, not treatment. I already have enough feedback from my own work and from people in my organization to know that this idea is feasible.

Finally, I think that, as is done in some schools, choice theory can be taught to both students and teachers and is helpful to all aspects of education. It also can be used to counsel people before marriage, since external control psychology destroys almost every marriage that fails.

For people who are interested in training in both reality therapy in action and choice theory, the William Glasser Institute is the only official source of this training. The institute trains people all over the world and can provide training locally to groups as small as ten people anywhere in the United States and Canada. The comprehensive three-week program is spaced over at least eighteen months, with study and practice between the weeks. It culminates in a certification week, and each trainee who completes the program gets a certificate.

For more detailed information on all the institute does, contact:

The William Glasser Institute
22024 Lassen Street, Suite 118
Chatsworth, CA 91311

Phone (818) 700-8000
Fax (818) 700-0555
E-mail wginst@earthlink.net
Web site http://www.wglasser.com

Postscript

Based on the 1965 book, *Reality Therapy,* this therapy is now practiced widely all over the world. My goal with *Counseling with Choice Theory* is to increase the spread of these ideas. To do this I would like to enlist your help in going beyond what I could show in this book. For example, the emotions in our voices, the expressions on our faces, the gestures we make with our hands and the pace of the conversations. The only way this additional information could be provided is to use the transcripts in this book as scripts and recreate the counseling sessions, as well as my comments, on videotape.

Since I have retained the audio and video rights, I will grant the right to videotape the sessions in this book to any interested individual or group for personal use. For example, a college counseling class could make a videotape of one or more sessions and use this tape to teach the ideas.

In exchange for this right, I would ask you to send a copy of the tape to the William Glasser Institute, where it would become institute property. We would review it and, if we believe it has merit, distribute it as widely as possible. Our whole purpose would be to make this material available at low cost to help spread the ideas. Any money we make would be used to support the nonprofit institute. No individual would profit personally from your gift.

In a college or university, this could be an interesting cooperative effort between the departments of Theater Arts and Counseling. Many colleges have state-of-the-art television facilities where the sessions could be produced. I would also encourage anyone who is a member of an interested theater group to do the same thing. It would be good practice and an opportunity for actors to add this tape to their résumés and showcase their acting skills to a wide audience.

Anyone interested should write the William Glasser Institute both for official permission and for further suggestions on how to proceed. If you believe in reality therapy, I urge you to use your creativity to promote these ideas. The tapes need not be restricted to the English language. We welcome all languages.

Index

Author photograph © Craig Ferré

William Glasser, M.D., is a world-renowned psychiatrist who lectures widely. The author of many books, including *Choice Theory, Reality Therapy, The Quality School,* and *Staying Together,* he is the president of the William Glasser Institute in Los Angeles. The Reverend Robert Schuller has called him "the world's greatest psychologist."

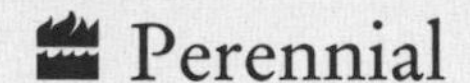

Books by William Glasser:

CHOICE THEORY
ISBN 0-06-093014-4
Dr. Glasser offers a non-controlling psychology to help sustain relationships.

THE LANGUAGE OF CHOICE THEORY
ISBN 0-06-095323-3
Real-life conversations. On the left-hand page is a typical controlling order or threat, and on the right a more reasonable version, using choice theory.

CHOICE THEORY IN THE CLASSROOM
ISBN 0-06-095287-3
Glasser puts his successful choice theory to work in our schools.

REALITY THERAPY
ISBN 0-06-090414-3
Glasser examines his alternative to Freudian psychoanalytic procedures, explains the procedure, and contrasts it to conventional treatment.

CONTROL THEORY IN THE PRACTICE OF REALITY THERAPY
ISBN 0-06-096400-6
A collection of case studies and examples of Control Theory in Reality Therapy.

THE CONTROL THEORY MANAGER
ISBN 0-887-30719-1 (HarperBusiness)
Glasser eplains what quality is and what managers need to do to achieve it.

THE QUALITY SCHOOL
ISBN 0-06-095286-5
An examination of coercive management in schools as an educational problem.

THE QUALITY SCHOOL TEACHER
ISBN 0-06-095285-7
Glasser shows how to establish warm, totally noncoercive relationships with students, teach only useful material, and promote student self-evaluation.

SCHOOLS WITHOUT FAILURE
ISBN 0-06-090421-6
Dr. Glasser offers daring recommendations to shake up educators.

POSITIVE ADDICTION
ISBN 0-06-091249-9
Glasser shows how to gain strength and self-esteem through positive behavior.

Available wherever books are sold, or call 1-800-331-3761 to order.